CELEBRATION OF
THE WORD

CELEBRATION OF THE WORD

Lucien Deiss, C.S.Sp.

Translated by Lucien Deiss, C.S.Sp.,
and Jane M.-A. Burton

A Liturgical Press Book

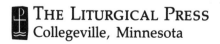

THE LITURGICAL PRESS
Collegeville, Minnesota

264.3
De C

Cover design by Greg Becker

Originally published in French by Desclée de Brouwer (*Célébration de la Parole*) in 1991.

Excerpts from the English translation of *The Roman Missal* copyright © 1973, 1985, International Committee on English in the Liturgy, Inc. (ICEL); excerpts from the *Liturgy of the Hours* © 1974, ICEL; excerpts from the *Lectionary for Mass* (second *editio typica*) © 1981, ICEL; excerpts from the *General Instruction of the Roman Missal* (second *editio typica*) from *Documents on the Liturgy, 1963–1979; Conciliar, Papal, and Curial Texts* © 1982, ICEL. All rights reserved.

The Scripture quotations contained in *Celebration of the Word* are the translation of the author.

1   2   3   4   5   6   7   8   9

Library of Congress Cataloging-in-Publication Data

Deiss, Lucien.
    [Célébration de la parole.   English]
    Celebration of the word / Lucien Deiss ; translated by Lucien
Deiss and Jane M.-A. Burton.
        p.   cm.
    Includes bibliographical references.
    ISBN 0-8146-2090-6
    1. Catholic Church—Liturgy.   2. Bible—Liturgical use.   3. Mass-
-Celebration.   I. Title.
BX1970.D3913   1993
264'.02—dc20   93-15193
                                                            CIP

Contents

Abbreviations

GIRM General Instruction on the Roman Missal, 1969

DC, Documentation Catholique

OLM, Ordo Lectionum Missae

SC, Collection *Sources chrétiennes*, Cerf

TWNT, Theologisches Wörterbuch zum Neuen Testament, Ed. Kohlhammer

PL Patrologia Latina, ed. J. P. Migne

Introduction

The word *celebration* evokes the image of a festive gathering. To celebrate the Word of God is to *hold a feast* around the Word.

When Ezra, returning from captivity in Babylon, gathered together the exiles in Jerusalem for a solemn reading of the Law—it was about the year 445, at the time of the feast of Tabernacles—all the assembly, with uplifted hands, cried out in response to the blessing pronounced in their name "Amen! Amen!," prostrated themselves, their faces to the ground in sign of adoration, and shed tears of joy on hearing the Word of God. Then, the reading completed, "all the people began to eat and drink, distributing the portions and giving themselves up to great rejoicing, for they had understood the words which had been proclaimed to them."[1]

More than twenty-five centuries have passed since that celebration. Our assemblies are less festive. Are we still able to "hold a feast" around the Word? What does such a celebration require today? And, first of all, why celebrate the Word? A community gathers on "the Lord's day" to celebrate the Risen Christ in the "Lord's Supper."[2] Is it really necessary to read the texts of the Old Testament, St. Paul's letters, and the Gospel pericopes?

A complementary question: if one wants to read texts, why not select readings from contemporary sources, more adapted to our contemporary mentality and sensibility?

Here we touch the heart of the problem. The essential question is not: how to proclaim the biblical readings (as well as possible),

[1] Neh 8:12.
[2] Rev 1:10; 1 Cor 11:20.

nor: what texts should we proclaim? (the Lectionary answers this question), but: why proclaim the Word of God in our celebrations? Many non-Christian religions use and chant sacred texts in their tradition. Hinduism possesses its Veda; Buddhism's rich legends concern the life and teaching of the Buddha; Islam has the Koran. What do we Christians, whom the Koran[3] is pleased to call "the people of the Scriptures," do when we proclaim the Bible in our assemblies? It is clear that we were not baptized in order to read the Scriptures, nor to listen to homilies, nor to make intercession in the prayer of the faithful, but rather to enter into a communion of life with the Risen Christ and to share that life, beyond the frontiers of death, in the infinity of eternity. What then is our aim in celebrating the Word of God? In other words, what is the "ministerial function"[4] of the biblical readings?

We have the ritual of reading the Bible in our celebrations. What does this serve?

This is a fundamental question of existence or non-existence, since it questions the very root of the ritual. For it is clear that if "this serves no point"—and this often happens in the rituals of many religions—or if it serves only the rite itself, then the axe of the question must chop off the rite at its root and throw it in the vast cemetery of past rites.

The stakes

Vatican II affirms: "It is by the force of the Gospel (*virtute evangelii*) that the Holy Spirit rejuvenates the Church and renews her incessantly."[5] The renewal of the Church, set in motion by the Council, takes root and draws its strength from the Word of God. Therefore, it is necessary that the Christian community, weighed down and grown old by the weight of institutions, should be continually renewed as a *biblical Church* by the eternal youthfulness of the Spirit.

---

[3] *The Koran*, V. 19.

[4] The expression "ministerial function" translates *munus ministeriale*, an expression used in the Constitution on the Sacred Liturgy, *Sacrosanctum Concilium*, 112. *Munus* (from which the adjective *ministerialis* is derived) signifies "function," "office." Each rite must accomplish its ministerial function, that is, the reason for it is carried out.

[5] Dogmatic Constitution on the Church, *Lumen Gentium*, 4.

What is a "biblical Church"? It is not a Church of biblicists, where the ideal is to make all the faithful into mini-exegetes. Ancient Jewish tradition dreamed of a paradise where the elect, inebriated by the chant of myriads of angels, would study the Torah without end.[6] Such is not the dream of Christians, neither for life in heaven nor for life on earth. A biblical Church is a Church built not on human traditions but on the Word of God, not on the sand of human norms but on the rock of divine laws, a Church fashioned according to God's own heart.

This was the project of the Council. Is it in process of being realized, or has it already been frustrated?[7]

It is not irreverent to ask such a question. A council, even one placed under the sign of the Spirit, is not necessarily a success. It may even be a total failure. History reminds us of the painful memory of the Fifth Lateran Council (1512–1517) at which Tommaso Giustiniani and Vincenzo Quirini of the Order of Camaldoli proposed a plan of radical and prophetic reform for the Church.[8] Alas, this plan was drowned by sermons of lyric flight, discussions of ecclesiastical precedence, and pious considerations, but without any real grasp of what needed to be reformed. "What dare I say of councils," asked Erasmus with irony, "except perhaps that the recent Lateran council has not been one."[9] On March 16, 1517, Pope Leo X closed this blocked council, and in October of the same year, Luther posted his theses at Wittenberg. In 1545, twenty-eight years too late, the Council of Trent began.

Lateran Council V could have been the Council of the Reformation. It did not know how to give a response to the problems of the age. Trent was the Council of the Counter-Reformation. Instead of a response, it resisted the problems. The price paid at Trent for the Lateran Council was the tearing apart of the Christian community into Catholics and Protestants. This was the price paid for the art of oratory which flourished at the Lateran.

[6] See L. Glinzberg, *The Legends of the Jews*, ed. Jewish Publication Society of America, Philadelphia, vol. 1, 1937, 21.

[7] See, for example, the acts of the International Colloquium of Bologna, 1980, in *Les Églises après Vatican II*, coll. "Théologie historique," 61, Beaushesne, 1981.

[8] For this subject, see O. De La Brosse, J. Leclerc, H. Holstein, C. Lefebvre, *Latran V et Trente*, coll. "Histoire des Conciles Oecuméniques," 10, Éd. de l'Orante, Paris, 1975.

[9] Erasmus, *Opus Epistolarum*, P. S. Allen, Oxford, V, 33, *Epist.* 1268. Cited in *Latran V et Trente, op. cit.*, 113.

Finally, let us note that many of the problems dealt with at Trent—those of the liturgy in particular!—were resolved at Vatican II, four centuries too late!

Is Vatican Council II to renew the unhappy experience of Lateran V? The answer is in the hands of each community. It is expressed in the effort of the community to become each day a more biblical community.

On this great adventure of the discovery of the riches of the Word, the Sunday Eucharistic celebration is certainly not the only celebration possible. All forms of biblical study and prayer, whether by individuals or by groups, are highly praiseworthy. Yet the Sunday Eucharistic celebration is the most important for the ecclesial community. For the Eucharist, is it not, according to Vatican II, "the summit of the Christian life,"[10] "the center of the Christian life"?[11]

Such are the stakes of the problem dealt with in the pages which follow.

After commenting on the riches and the imperfections of the present Lectionary (chapter 1), we shall consider the relationship between the celebration and the Word and the celebration of the Covenant as the fundamental part of our study (chapter 2). We shall speak of the Responsorial Psalm, which is normally the only sung reading in our Eucharistic celebrations (chapter 3), of the Homily which actualizes the Word (chapter 4), and of the Prayer of the Faithful which responds to it (chapter 5), the actors in the celebration of the Word (chapter 6), and lastly, the objects, places and rites which make up the ritual environment (chapter 7). We shall conclude by a brief balance-sheet and some expectations.

---

[10] Dogmatic Constitution on the Church, *Lumen Gentium*, 11.
[11] Decree on the Ministry and Life of Priests, *Presbyterorum Ordinis*, 5.

1
The Lectionary's Riches and Imperfections

BIRTH OF THE NEW LECTIONARY

In the Constitution on the Sacred Liturgy (51), Vatican II asked that "the treasures of the Bible be opened up more lavishly for the faithful."

Clearly, it was a question of reforming and renewing the Lectionary, the liturgical book that contains the readings from the Word of God. This reform affected not only the texts proclaimed in the Eucharistic celebration on Sundays and holydays (Lectionary for Sundays and Feasts) and the Weekday Masses (Weekday Lectionary), but also the proposed readings for the celebration of the sacraments.

The "Consilium"[1] for the implementation of the reforms of Vatican II started to work from the end of the Council in 1965. The official Latin edition of the *Ordo Lectionum Missae* that proposed the new readings appeared May 25, 1969, on the feast of Pentecost. The decree that promulgated it began:

> The Constitution on the Sacred Liturgy directed that the treasures of the Bible be opened up more lavishly so that a richer share might be provided for the faithful at the table of God's word and

[1] Official title: *Consilium ad exsequendam Constitutionem de Sacra Liturgia* (Consilium for the Implementation of the Constitution on the Sacred Liturgy).

a more representative portion of sacred Scripture be read to the people over a prescribed number of years (article 51). In response to these directives, the Consilium for the Implementation of the Constitution on the Liturgy prepared this Lectionary for Mass and Pope Paul VI approved it in the apostolic constitution *Missale Romanum,* 3 April 1969.

Such was the official birth of our present Lectionary. The "newborn" was officially welcomed by the Catholic community of the Latin Rite on November 30, 1969, the first Sunday of Advent.

Since that date the Lectionary has grown in the midst of Christian assemblies. The act of birth could predict nothing of its destiny. We thought that it would be rich. In fact, the Lectionary has revealed its multiple strengths. It constitutes the principal newness of the reformed Mass. It has also revealed certain imperfections.

STRUCTURE OF THE LECTIONARY

The structure of the biblical texts presented by the Lectionary is well known. Here is a simple reminder.

Lectionary for Sundays and Feasts

The Masses of the Lectionary for Sundays and Feasts include three readings (four if, according to tradition, one counts the Responsorial Psalm as a reading):

• *The first* is from the Old Testament, except during the Easter season when it is taken from the Acts of the Apostles.

• *The second* is from "the Apostle," that is, from the letters of the "Pauline Corpus,"[2] or from the Book of Revelation, according to the liturgical season.

• *The third* is from the Gospel.

In order to have variety and an abundance of biblical texts, the readings are distributed over three years or a cycle.

[2] By Pauline corpus, is understood all the letters attributed to Paul, including the letters whose authorship is disputed. According to R. E. Brown, "as a very large approximation," 90 percent of exegetes call into doubt the Pauline authorship of the Pastorals (the two letters to Timothy and the Letter to Titus); 80 percent the letter to the Ephesians, and 60 percent, the Letter to the Colossians (*The Churches the Apostles Left Behind,* New York: Paulist, 1984).

The cycles are designated by the letters A, B, and C. Cycle C, the third, is used in the years whose date is divisible by three. The liturgical year begins, according to the tradition of the Latin rite, on the First Sunday of Advent.

The second reading as well as the third—that of the Gospel—is continuous or semi-continuous.[3] The first, on the contrary, does not follow any principle of continuity. It is chosen simply in terms of the Gospel. The Responsorial Psalm is a response to the first reading.

Here, for example, are the readings of the Thirty-First Sunday of Year B:

First Reading (non-continuous):
   Deuteronomy 6:2-6: "You shall love the Lord your God with all your heart . . . ."

Responsorial Psalm:
   Psalm 18: "I love you, O Lord, my strength."

Second Reading (semi-continuous):
   Letter to the Hebrews 7:23-28.
   (Reading of the preceding Sunday: Heb 5:1-6.
   Reading of the following Sunday: Heb 9:24-28).

Third Reading (semi-continuous):
   Gospel according to Mark 12:28-34: The commandment of love: "You shall love the Lord your God . . . ."
   (Reading of the preceding Sunday: Mark 10:46-52.
   Reading of the following Sunday: Mark 12:38-44).

This structure is particularly affirmed for Sundays in Ordinary Time. On feasts and in the major liturgical seasons (Advent, Lent and Eastertide), the readings are chosen rather by theme, according to the meaning of the liturgical time.

The intention is to manifest "the unity of the two Testaments and of the history of salvation, "in which Christ is the central figure, commemorated in his paschal mystery."[4]

---

[3] In a continuous or semi-continuous reading, one follows the order of the chapters and verses; in a continuous reading, the entire text is read; in a semi-continuous reading, extracts are read.

[4] *Ordo Lectionum Missae,* §66. We quote from the second edition (January 21, 1981), which develops considerably, in its "Praenotanda," the theology of the Word of God in the liturgical celebration. This theology had only been outlined in the first edition of 1969.

Finally, let us note that the structure of the readings is underlined with a certain ritual elegance. The first two readings are followed by an intercalary song and the third—the Gospel—by the
Homily and the Prayer of the Faithful. There is a dialogue between
the Word coming from God and the word rising toward God from
the community:

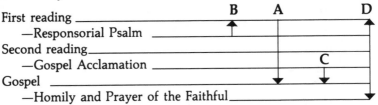

First reading
  —Responsorial Psalm
Second reading
  —Gospel Acclamation
Gospel
  —Homily and Prayer of the Faithful

This structure is rather fascinating on the intellectual level. The
first reading announces the Gospel (A), the Psalm points back to
the first reading (B), the Acclamation prefaces the Gospel (C), the
Homily and the Prayer of the Faithful weld together the unity of
the whole (D). The equilibrium of the celebration is disturbed somewhat if the first or second reading is omitted.

Weekday Lectionary

The Weekday Lectionary presents two semi-continuous readings with the Responsorial Psalm which "responds" to the first reading. It unfolds in a two-year cycle.

RICHES OF THE NEW LECTIONARY

The riches of the Lectionary since Vatican II are incontestable:
the Christian people once again have the good fortune to have access, at the very heart of the liturgical celebration, to the riches of
the Bible. The Lectionary could even be considered as a "mini-Bible"
for the use of the whole Christian people and, indeed, has occasionally been published as such.[5]
  Certainly, all the faithful can read their Bibles individually or
in the family circle. Such has been the long practice of Christian

[5] See *La Bible, Traduction officielle de la Liturgie. Texte complet du Lectionnaire,*
ed. Desclée de Brouwer, Droguet-Ardent (1st edition, 1973).

piety, and especially of Protestant piety, at a time when Latin formed a barrier between the community and the Word. One can also study it among friends in a Bible study group. But today, the Council offers the Christian people a new and abundant reading of Scripture that is at the very heart of the liturgical celebration itself.

Perhaps one could criticize the Lectionary for too great a richness. How can all the biblical texts of a single Sunday Mass be explained and celebrated? One might as well reproach a bride for being too beautiful! It is Christian wisdom to take profitably what one reasonably can from this wealth, but also to avoid the excesses that could harm the spiritual health of the community. Just as it is unwise to give a hungry person too much rich food and cause indigestion, so too it is unwise to inflict biblical indigestion on our communities by gorging them with texts. Even in spiritual matters, it is proper to keep a sane equilibrium. It suffices to choose, and everyone knows that it is easier to choose when there is an abundance.

REGRETS

Certain imperfections, while regrettable, are normal. It is clear that a reform that abandons lectionaries that fifteen centuries of Christian tradition have devised[6] and which exposes itself voluntarily to the impetuous breath of the Holy Spirit cannot avoid certain imperfections. It had been thought that the boat of the Church would allow itself to be pushed gracefully by the gentle breeze of the Spirit according to a wisely direct reform. But the tornado of renewal has thrown the boat far out into the biblical ocean.

Here are a few remarks.

A difficult "symphony"

We said earlier that the pericopes of the Old Testament had been chosen to parallel to some degree the Gospel of each Sunday. This is an excellent idea, but the result is sometimes disappointing.

---

[6] The oldest lectionaries seem to go back to the middle of the fifth century. Cf. A. G. Martimort, *The Church in Prayer*, vol. 1, Collegeville: The Liturgical Press, 1987.

It is not clear that each pericope from the Gospels can be suitably illustrated by a pericope from the Old Testament. In any case, the choice of the texts from the Old Testament does not always take into account what tradition proudly called the ecclesial symphony of the two choirs of the Old and New Testaments.[7] Two melodies can be ravishing in beauty and intoxicating in rhythm. Put together, they do not necessarily form a two-part harmony.

The editors of the Lectionary also wanted to include all the books of the Old Testament. Yet it is not evident that the pericopes chosen as prefaces to the Gospel readings present the best face of Old Testament revelation.

Parcelling out the books of the Old Testament

Above all, it is regrettable that the books of the Old Testament are cut up in fragments that no longer have links between them and that wander like orphans in the immense forest of biblical tradition. One illustrates the New Testament in this way, but one loses the face of the Old. Its dynamism is veiled. One no longer perceives the formidable history of the People of God that originates in the call of Abraham in Ur of the Chaldees and that in Jesus of Nazareth touches the shores of eternity. In beginning the history of the People of the Promise, God inaugurated an eternal history that would be a river of both holiness and sin flowing into the ocean of divinity.

Do our Old Testament readings, appropriately called "pericopes," that is to say cuttings, which, at the mercy of each Sunday, wander from century to century, sometimes before David, sometimes after him, give the impression of a holy history which progresses in the *fullness of time*[8] toward Jesus? How can we recognize this in the cycle of the Patriarchs from Genesis 12 to 22, for example, when the readings are scattered over three years in five different places?[9] As for the Jacob cycle (Gen 25:19 to 50:14), the Sunday Lectionary does not even mention him![10] How can we recog-

---

[7] See H. De Lubac, *Exégèse Mediévale*, coll. "Theologie," 41, 1959, 328–329.

[8] Gal 4:4.

[9] On the second Sunday of Lent, A, B, and C; at the Easter vigil; on the Feast of Corpus Christi, C; and on the sixteenth and seventeenth Sundays, C.

[10] The faithful of the Sunday assemblies will therefore know nothing about Jacob's ladder which descended from heaven to earth and upon which the angels joined the kingdom of heaven to our earth (Gen 28:10-17). It is true that they will also not know

nize Jeremiah as the prophet with a heart of fire, when the flaming torches of his prophecies are dispersed over three years in the meadow of the Sunday liturgy?[11] Jeremiah should have rekindled the community, illuminated its darkness, and made it cherish the marvelous prophet whom Yahweh had "seduced."[12] The prophets appear in Israel's sky like a shower of stars: they sparkle intermittently like those luminous signs that switch off as soon as they are lit. They are like dawns that do not reach full day. They can only partially illuminate the sky of our Sunday celebrations. Let us say clearly: the community has no serious chance of making continuous contact with the message of the books of the Old Testament through the Lectionary for Sundays and Feasts.[13]

Proper value of the Old Testament

It is regrettable moreover that the Sunday Lectionary does not underline with more clarity the proper value of the Old Testament. The Old Testament does not just validate the New; it possesses its own spiritual value. David is not only a type of Jesus, but truly his ancestor according to God's plan. And just as Jesus is born of his flesh, "of the seed of David," (ἐκ τοῦ σπέρματος Δαυίδ), as Scripture[14] says so forcefully, so the message of the Gospel is born in the spiritual tradition of the Davidic people. In like manner, the commandment of love according to Deuteronomy is not only a prophecy of the New Law of the Gospel. Here it is rather the New Testament which borrows from the Old. One might say that it is the old that is new, and that the new copies the old. And this commandment, "which is not a new commandment but an old com-

---

that the Covenant with Jacob is fulfilled in Jesus upon whom "the angels of heaven ascend and descend (John 1:51), for this text no longer appears in the Sunday Lectionary.

[11] On the twelfth and twenty-second Sundays, A; on the twelfth Sunday, B; on the fourth and sixth Sundays, C.

[12] Jer 20:7.

[13] This difficulty has little importance for the books that have no internal unity (because they are themselves made up of various fragments). But it plays an important role for the books that possess a certain internal unity and whose oracles are complete and balanced. Let one think, for example, of the minor prophets, of Deutero-Isaiah, of Trito-Isaiah, etc. A clear understanding of the Word is then rendered singularly more difficult.

[14] John 7:42.

mandment,"[15] is perfect in itself. It contains the whole Law, the Prophets, and the Gospel.[16] The New Testament can add nothing to it except Jesus alone, who has observed the commandment of Deuteronomy in its fullness. We must now imitate that fullness.

In order to do justice to the scriptural reality, it is necessary to speak of the Old Testament as the First Covenant, and of the New as the last Covenant (*novissimum Testamentum*), the ultimate, definitive Covenant.[17]

Certainly the First Covenant contained elements which had grown old and were thus destined to disappear.[18] Yet it also expressed decisive revelations about God which the New Covenant does not surpass. For example, when the New Testament affirms that God is love, it is only summing up the sublime revelations about the God of tenderness and mercy which are at the heart of Israel's tradition.

Is the value of the Old Testament, which is broken up into short readings in the service of the Gospel, thus placed in full light? The message of God is a torrent of tenderness. Distilled drop by drop on Sundays, has it not lost the freshness of its impetuosity?

The problem of the Pauline Corpus

We saw previously that the Pauline Corpus[19] is well represented in the new Lectionary by the second reading. This reading is semi-continuous. Preferential treatment is given therefore to Paul's Letters. But in practice, the celebration of the Word does not always do them justice.

The Gospel, the reading from the Old Testament which prefaces it, and the Responsorial Psalm which responds to the first reading present a certain thematic unity. The temptation is therefore great to take this unity as the preponderant theme of the Homily. Many

---

[15] 1 John 2:7-8.

[16] Cf. Matt 22:40.

[17] Cf. les "Orientations pastorales du Comité français pour les relations avec le judaïsme": "The first Covenant, in fact, was not nullified by the new one. It is the root and source of it, the foundation and the promise" (D. C., vol. 70 (1973), 421). See also F. Mussner, *Traktat über die Juden*, München, Kösel-Verlag, 1979 (French translation: *Traité sur les Juifs*, Coll. "Cogitatio fidei," 109, Paris, Editions du Cerf, 1981, and the remarks of P. Benoit in *Revue Biblique*, 1982, 588–595.

[18] Heb 8:13.

[19] Cf. note 2.

communities easily succumb to this temptation without any trace of malice nor shadow of intellectual laziness. Paul's message, which does not accommodate itself to the other biblical texts, is not sufficiently emphasized. Poor Paul! He is marvelous, sometimes sublime. But there are no more jewelry boxes in which to place the pearls that he offers: we have used them all for the Gospel. It is only occasionally, when his text accords somewhat with the theme of the Gospel, that Paul furnishes the subject for the Homily.

Number of readings

As we said above, an abundance of biblical pericopes to read is better than penury, for it allows a choice. This is certainly true, but only when the choice is discretionary, as in Sunday assemblies without a priest. This is not the case in the celebration of the Word at Mass. *Volens, nolens,* the community is obliged to take what is given. It must read all the texts, even those for which it does not hunger, and those which, for lack of time, neither the Homily nor the Prayer of the Faithful will be able to actualize.

Some communities have reduced the number of readings to two. They omit the first or the second reading. Such a decision is always difficult to make in individual cases—even if it is imposed by lack of time when Sunday Masses follow each other very closely.[20] Whenever made, it creates a certain uneasiness. The priest who presides at the Eucharist is not the "proprietor" of the Word, as if he had the right to choose the texts as he thinks fit. He cannot "enchain" the Word[21] in silence, even for a motive that he himself considers valid. He is simply a "steward of the mysteries of God." As a steward ($οἰκονόμος$), he administers ($οἰκονομεῖ$) the house of God. "For all that one asks of stewards is that they be found faithful."[22] His first fidelity consists in distributing the Word in its integrity which has been entrusted to him. May he be a "faithful dispenser of the Word of truth."[23] It is precisely for this purpose that he presides at the Eucharist.

[20] The decision to reduce the readings to two can be made by the episcopal Conference. In that case "one will take care to never choose a text simply because it is shorter or easier" (*General Instruction of the Roman Missal,* §318).
[21] Cf. 2 Tim 2:9.
[22] 1 Cor 4:1-2.
[23] 2 Tim 2:15.

And if the reading that he decided to omit were precisely that which certain members of the faithful needed, and that the Church had provided for their hunger that Sunday, what weight of responsibility would he take upon himself!

But if in reading all the texts, one walks at ease on the straight path of obedience to liturgical laws, and thus conscientiously fulfills one's vocation of steward, one finds oneself confronted with another problem. Since everything must be read, one reads everything, but one does not celebrate everything. For lack of time, one no longer actualizes the Word in the Homily; one no longer responds to it in the Prayer of the Faithful. The proclamation of the Word is reduced to the level of a simple rubric. Certainly, the rubric is kept. But at what price? To sacrifice the Word to the rubric is too high a price to pay for the rubric!

This problem of the number of readings presents itself even at weekday Masses. It is sometimes difficult to celebrate the Word well—the first reading, the Responsorial Psalm and the Gospel—in the Homily and the Prayer of the Faithful when this Word is abundant. It is not the quantity of texts read which is important but the quality of the celebration, the quality of the encounter between the celebrating community and God who speaks to it.

Were other, better solutions possible?

The members of the Consilium on the Liturgy who selected the readings made the best possible choice following the decisions of the Council. It is not the chosen readings that may be criticized, but the terms in which the problem had been posed and the solutions reached, that is, the decision to keep three readings and the Responsorial Psalm for each Sunday and two readings and the Responsorial Psalm for the weekday Masses.

Were there different solutions which would have been better and which would have introduced the faithful more efficaciously to the riches of the Word? I doubt it. As long as the Christian community comes together only once a week, during the short hour of the Sunday Mass, and consecrates only a small part of that time to the meditation of the Word, it closes the door to a full knowledge of the Word.

Let us say it clearly: To acquire that knowledge which satisfies the intelligence and inflames the heart, it is necessary to pay the price for it. Are Christians ready, as individuals, to make use of their Bible as a book of prayer and study? Is the Christian community ready to do it by gathering together around the Word more than once a week? Is it ready to renounce Sunday minimalism? One secures one's soul on the plane of legalism. Is it sufficient to satisfy one's heart? Is a love which is spoken only once a week—and then for just an instant—sufficient to maintain a flame? Is a Word which is listened to only once a week sufficient to nourish a dialogue and animate an exchange? We cannot run away from these questions. The strength and the joy of our faith depend on its deep-rootedness in the Word. And it is on the quality of our faith that the quality of our witness before the world depends.

Allow me a personal recollection. I was in Guyana, at Sinnamary. With the Franciscan Sisters of Mary, I went to visit a leper who lived alone in a hut of rotten wood only two by three meters big. The hands and feet of the poor woman in her fifties had been consumed by the terrible disease, and she found herself nailed on her bed of planks waiting for someone to visit her and help her. And yet she still found a way to share the food brought to her with those poorer than she. I asked her, "Idole, how do you pass such long days and nights alone?" She answered me, "Father, I am busy all the time. In the morning I do my housework. (What could she do except arrange her pillow?) Then, right away, I take up the Gospel. And then, I am fully involved in God's affairs!" I said "Idole, I bring you Jesus' blessing. Stay always fully involved in God's affairs!" In her swollen face, her large black eyes wept with joy. And while I was blessing her, I thought to myself that I was seeing realized before me the word of the Psalm:

> How I love your law, O Lord,
> all day long I meditate on it!
> Your Word gives light
> and the simple understand it (Pss 119, 97, 130).

Idole died a few months later. Thus she entered forever "fully into God's affairs." I will never forget her big eyes that seemed to smile at heaven when she spoke of the Gospel.

We end here our remarks on the Lectionary. Our intention was neither to praise nor to blame. We should simply like to remain lucid. Of course, it is not a question of lucidity in our love for the Word of God. In that love we willingly accept to be seduced, amazed with wonder! If only the Word could fascinate us, if the splendor of Jesus, Word of God, could burn our heart to its roots! But here, it is simply a question of the Lectionary. We do not want to confuse our loving regard for the Word of God with our look at the Lectionary.

Having said this, we will adopt the following wise course: the Council gave a new Lectionary to the Latin Rite. This is a unique opportunity. How can we now use this treasure to best benefit for the whole Christian community? As people of the faith, we inherit the divine Word: whatever the burdens and inherent difficulties of entering into possession of this heritage may be, how can we make it bear fruit? How can we best resolve, in triple fidelity to tradition, to present rubrics, and to the celebrating community, the problems that can arise?

2
Celebration of the Word
and Celebration of the Covenant

This chapter tackles the fundamental question: what exactly is the ministerial function of the celebration of the Word? Why do we Christians celebrate the Word? What is the goal we hope to reach through this celebration?

THE "EXTREME IMPORTANCE" OF THE WORD OF GOD

Vatican II affirms that "in the celebration of the liturgy, holy Scripture is of extreme importance (*maximum momentum*)."[1] Can we define the nature of this importance? The expression "extreme importance," despite its emphasis, remains vague. A reality may perhaps be extremely important in a human life, without thereby effecting that life by being at its root.

The Creative Word

The Word of God is the *root* of all that exists, in particular of the universe of love that is the ecclesial community. The Word is important in the same way that the Word which called the universe into existence is "important." "God spoke and the world was. God

[1] Constitution on the Sacred Liturgy, *Sacrosanctum Concilium*, 24.

commanded and the world existed."[2] This Word, that causes everything to exist, from the tiny daisy to the billions of stars and galax-
ies, also calls into existence the spiritual universe that is the new
heavens and the new earth.

Just as in the Old Testament, God chose Israel, a people that
did not exist, from among the nations, establishing it as a "first-
born child."[3] And just as God called into existence the Church, the
Body of Christ, his first-born child, so God continues today to call
into existence, by his creative Word, ecclesial communities. Vatican II affirms: "Particular churches are born of the Word."[4] "It is
the Word of salvation which awakens faith in the hearts of non-
Christians, which nourishes faith in the hearts of Christians, which
gives birth and growth to Christian communities."[5] God creates
everything by his Word, "the visible and invisible universe."[6] Thus
God also creates by his Word the spiritual universe that is the salvation of human beings.

The Creation continues

This creative activity of God is not confined to a unique creative event, which God realizes once and for all "in the beginning."
As if God, after having taken the earth in the palm of his hand,
abandoned it afterwards, throwing it into the blind round of centuries. Creation is being created at each moment. "Creation is being effected today. It is not finished. Humanity is a genesis, a
permanent growth. Today is the day of Creation."[7] Creation receives
its being as a permanent gift from God. If God did not hold, at
each moment, the mountains and the abysses in his hand, they
would fall into nothingness. If God did not kindle, at each moment,
the light at the heart of the darkness, the earth would turn upside
down in the night. There is not, each day, any implied renewal of
existence. Each dawn is a gift from God.

With reason Jewish piety, in its morning prayer, blesses the Creator thus: "You are blessed, Lord our God, King of the universe

[2] Ps 33:9.
[3] Exod 4:22.
[4] Decree on the Missionary Activity of the Church, *Ad Gentes*, 6.
[5] Decree on the Ministry and Life of Priests, *Presbyterorum Ordinis*, 4.
[6] Col 1:16.
[7] P. Ganne, *La Création* (Éditions du Cerf, 1979) 11.

. . . who out of goodness, constantly renew every day the works of your creation."[8]

If God continues at each instant to create the visible and invisible universe, God also continues at each instant, to create the believing community. The community exists only to the degree that it welcomes day by day this Word which guards it from disintegrating into nothingness and keeps it from the abyss.[9]

Jewish tradition has expressed well this continual necessity of being rooted in the lifegiving power of the Word. We know that the synagogal office used to be celebrated all Mondays and Thursdays as well as on the Sabbath, thus three times a week.[10] Allegorizing on the text of Exodus 15:22: "They walked in the desert for three days and did not find any water," the doctors of the law explained with tenderness: "The water designates nothing other than the Torah[11] itself, according to Isaiah 55:1: 'O you who are thirsty, come to the water.' When they had wandered for three days without the instruction of the Torah, they were exhausted. The prophets then rose up in their midst and ordered the reading of the Torah on the Sabbath; one had then to skip the first day of the week (=Sunday), read again, skip again the third and fourth days to read again on the fifth (=Thursday), and skip finally the day of preparation (=Friday). Thus one would not remain for more than three days without the reading of the Torah."[12] In the desert of that life, the celebration of the Word was like an oasis. It would open to the pilgrims of the Exodus a way to the source of living water. It allowed them to survive day after day and to reach the Promised Land.

A listening unceasingly renewed

Such a listening to the Word is renewed unceasingly. One has never finished discovering the ways of God nor marveling at the paths of God's love. No one can say: "I know the Bible sufficiently."

---

[8] Blessing which accompanies the recitation of the *Shema Israel* (Deut 6:4-9). See L. Deiss, *The Springtime of the Liturgy*, Collegeville, The Liturgical Press, 1979, 15.

[9] Cf. OLM 47.

[10] Megillah, 3, 6 and 4, 1. See H. Danby, *The Mishnah*, Oxford University Press, 1967, 205-206.

[11] *Torah* means here the five books of the Pentateuch.

[12] Strack-Billerbeck, *Kommentar zum Neuen Testament aus Talmud und Midrasch*, Ed. C. H. Beck, München, 1961, 155.

Even if a person knew it by heart to the last verse, he or she could not say it. Why?

Of course, the Word does not change. But we change at each moment; our joys and our pains, our hopes and our anxieties, and therefore our position before the Word. Each day of our existence, the commandment "You shall love the Lord your God with all your heart"[13] unveils new horizons, opens new paths before us, makes new appeals resound in the silence of our peace. Each morning that God makes for us, God also creates a new heart to listen to him. Each morning that God opens the doors of dawn, God also opens the ear of his servants:

> Every morning, he awakens my ear
> so that I may listen like his disciple.[14]

Nothing then is more changing than this old immutable Bible, nothing is more unforseeable than these old oracles two and three thousand years old, nothing is younger than these old texts which each morning invent new demands for us and reveal God's ever-new mercies.

WORD AND EUCHARIST

The Word has the same importance as the Eucharist

Can we clarify even more this "extreme importance" of the Word? Yes. In affirming that the Word of God is of exactly the same importance as the Eucharist.

Such an affirmation may surprise us. Is not devotion towards the Eucharist, of necessity, incomparable? Has not Christian devotion always been drawn to the Blessed Sacrament? We should not dare to advance such an affirmation if it were not the explicit teaching of the Council. Vatican II affirms:

> The Church had always venerated the holy Scriptures as she has venerated the Body of the Lord; she does not cease, especially in the holy Liturgy, to take the bread of life from the table of the Word

---

[13] Deut 6:5.
[14] Isa 50:4. Cf. Lam 3:23; Zeph 3:5.

and from the table of the Body of Christ, in order to offer it to the faithful.[15]

The Word of God is thus just as worthy of veneration as the Eucharistic Body of Christ Jesus. The one who "communicates" in the Word, like the one who communicates in the Eucharist, communicates in the same Lord. And the veneration due to the Word, like that due to the Eucharist, is the very veneration due to Christ Jesus.

In fact, the teaching of Vatican II, which may surprise us, also surprised certain of the Council fathers. Several amendments were proposed to the conciliar text. It was criticized for "assimilating too closely" (*nimis assimilare*) Word and Eucharist.[16] It was feared that the veneration of the Word would overshadow devotion to the Eucharist. These amendments were all justly rejected, for the Council simply took up the unwavering teaching of Christian theology and tradition.

The real presence of Christ in the Word and in the Eucharist

Both the mystery of the Word and the mystery of the Eucharist send one back to the mystery of Christ Jesus. They have the same importance in the sense that they are both epiphanies of the Risen One. Jerome (419–420) seems to delight in the jest of throwing confusion between Word and Eucharist when he explains:

> For my own part, I think that the Gospel is the Body of Christ and that the Holy Scriptures are his teaching. When the Lord speaks of eating his flesh and of drinking his blood, this may certainly be understood as referring to the mystery [of the Eucharist]. However, the Word of the Scriptures and his teaching are [also] his true body and his true blood.[17]

These are numerous meeting points between the mystery of the Word and that of the Eucharist:

Here, Christ is present under the "veil" of human words. There, he is present under the "veil" of bread and wine. Here, the Spirit

---

[15] Dogmatic Constitution on Divine Revelation, *Dei Verbum*, 15.

[16] See A. Grillmeier, *La Sainte Écriture dans la vie de L'Église*, in *La Révélation Divine*, coll. "Unam Sanctam," 70, 439.

[17] *In Isaiam Prologus. Corpus christianorum*, Series latina, vol. 63, 1. Cf. also H. De Lubac, *Exégèse Médiévale*, coll. "Théologie," 41, 1959, 522–524.

transfigures human words into inspired words, taking them up into the superior realm of Revelation, placing them in the treasury of the Word of God. There, this same Spirit, in the liturgical epiclesis, consecrates bread and wine into the body and blood of Christ, taking them up into the realm of creation transfigured by the divine.

Here, the Resurrection of Jesus, brought about by the Spirit, becomes the primary key for understanding the Scriptures. There, this same Resurrection gives its full meaning to the Eucharist, body of the Risen Christ and sacrament of Easter life. Lastly, here this Word becomes agent of eternal life. "You have the words of eternal life,"[18] is the cry of Christian faith in Christ Jesus. There, this same living bread descended from heaven, turns back the frontiers of death and gives eternal life.[19] Ignatius of Antioch writes, "Break this very bread, this bread which is the remedy of immortality, antidote against dying, bread of eternal life."[20]

The same presence of Christ which abides in the Scriptures also abides in the Eucharist. One may speak justly of the real presence of Christ in the Word, a presence just as real as that in the Eucharist. In his encyclical, *Mysterium fidei*, which centers on the Eucharist, and which justly insists on the real presence of Christ in the Eucharist, Paul VI explains that the real presence in the Eucharist does not exclude other modes of real presence:

> This presence one calls real, not in any exclusive sense, as if the other presences were not real, but, *par excellence*, because it is substantial.[21]

There is therefore, a real presence of Christ in the Eucharist, a presence which is substantial, *par excellence*, but there is also a real presence of Christ in his Word, which is likewise "real." Let us clarify these statements.

The real presence of Christ is called substantial: it is tied to the substance of the bread. On the one hand, it remains for as long as the Eucharistic celebration lasts, and, even after the celebration, for as long as the "species" of bread lasts. On the other hand, in the celebration of the Word, the real presence of Christ lasts for as long as the celebration of the Word continues, but it ceases when

---

[18] John 6:68.
[19] John 6:51.
[20] Ignatius of Antioch, *Letter to the Ephesians*, 20.
[21] *Mysterium Fidei* (3 September 1965) 39. Cf. also *Eucharistum Mysterium*, 9 (25 May 1967).

the celebration finishes and the assembly disperses. Yet, in both cases, the presence of Christ is a real presence.[22]

The two tables

Christian tradition has loved to speak of the two tables which allow us to communicate in Christ, the table of the Word and the table of the Eucharist. The Word is thus conceived as nourishment in the same way as the Eucharist. Commenting on the miracle of the multiplication of the loaves, Ambrose of Milan explains:

> This bread which Jesus breaks is, according to the mystery, the Word of God and a teaching about Christ. When this bread is distributed, it multiplies . . . Jesus gives his words as bread.[23]

The *Imitation of Christ* (fifteenth century) summarizes the whole of Christian tradition:

> You have given this poor, sick one, your sacred flesh as the food of his soul and body, and your Word as a lamp for his steps. I cannot live without these two things, for the Word of God is the light of the soul and your sacrament the bread of life.
>
> We may regard them as two tables set before the treasures of the Church. One is the table of the holy altar on which rests a blessed bread, the precious Body of the Lord. The other is the table of the divine law . . . which leads us securely, right into the Holy of Holies.[24]

Lastly, we know that Vatican II took up again the tradition of the two tables:

> The Church does not cease . . . to take the bread of life from the table of the Word and from the table of the Body of Christ.[25]
>
> Christians nourish themselves at the two tables of the Bible and the Eucharist.[26]

[22] The golden rule of sacramentalism is formulated thus by Saint Thomas: "While the species of bread and wine remain, the Body and Blood of Christ remains" (*Summa Theologica*, IIIa, pars, q. 77, art. 5).

[23] *Treatise on Luke's Gospel*, 6:86.

[24] *Imitation of Jesus Christ*, 4.11.

[25] *Dei Verbum*, 21.

[26] *Presbyterorum Ordinis*, 18. Cf. also *Perfectae Caritatis*, 6,*Ad Gentes*, 6. See also, W. Vogels, "La Parole de Dieu comme nourriture," in *La Pâque du Christ, mystère de Salut*, coll. "Lectio Divina," 111, Cerf, 1982, 33–50.

This theology of the two tables did not appear as an unprecedented shoot in the garden of the Church. On the contrary, it plunged its roots deeply into the depths of the biblical terrain. Already, towards the middle of the eighth century, the prophet Amos had spoken of a hunger for the word which would grip the people like a hunger for food.[27] Reflecting on the miracle of the manna, Deuteronomy discovered under the sign of bread, a search for the Word which would make one truly live:

> The Lord made you feel hunger, he gave you the manna to eat which neither you nor your fathers had known, in order to show you that human beings do not live only on bread, but on every word that comes from the mouth of God (Deut 8:3).

At the dawn of the Christian era, the author of the Book of Wisdom, surveying all the history of the chosen people, saw in this "bread of angels"[28] the sweetness that filled the children of God. And he adds:

> It is thus, Lord, that your beloved children would learn that it is your word which keeps those who believe in you.[29]

The comparison between Word and bread was familiar to Philo of Alexandria (†45). Commenting on the miracle of the manna, he wrote:

> Moses said to the Israelites: This is the bread that the Lord has given us to eat. It is the word given by the Lord. You see in what the food of the soul consists: the Word of God . . . This bread which he has given us to eat is this word.[30]

These themes, as one may suspect, are found in full flower in the Gospel accounts. Mark notes that before multiplying the loaves (Mark 6:34-44), Jesus multiplies the Word: "And he set himself to teach them at length" (6:34). Satisfying the people's hunger with the Word precedes satisfying it with bread. Israel waited for the messianic era when the miracle of the manna would be renewed: like Moses, Jesus led his people to the desert (6:35); like Moses, he

---

[27] Amos 8:11.
[28] Wis 16:20.
[29] Wis 16:26. See also Prov. 9:1-5, Sir 24:19-21.
[30] *Legum Allegoriae*, III, 169, 173. Cf. also, *De Sacrificiis*, 86, *De Fuga et Inventione*, 137.

made the assembly sit down in groups of fifty and of a hundred (6:40; cf. Exod 18:25); lastly, like Moses, he fed his own with a miraculous bread. This is the messianic feast with his own. The multiplied bread and the gift of the messianic law replace the manna of the Exodus and the gift of the Law on Sinai.[31]

The vocation of Jesus, like that of Israel, was an exodus, a march across the desert of his passion towards the promised land of the Resurrection.[32] His own bread was to do the will of the Father. Bread and Word, both gifts of heaven, are brought together in a loving obedience to his Father: "My food is to do the will of the one who sent me."[33]

The vicissitudes of history

We may ask how such a traditional teaching could have been lost in recent centuries in the moving sands of the collective memory.

It must be understood that the weight of theological discussions inherited from the past weighed heavily on certain questions, especially those concerned with the real presence of Christ in the Eucharist. Contemporary problems, which took all the attention of the age, finished by casting into the shadows a whole area of the theological landscape. This resulted in a lack of balance in the thought and sensibility of Christians.

In the face of questions and discussions on the Eucharist and its celebration, discussions which arose principally from the altercations between Ratrammus († c. 868) and Radbertus (†856), the polemics of Berengerius (†1088), then Wycliff (†1384), and finally from the sixteenth-century Reformation, Catholic theology hotly insisted on the real presence of Christ in the Eucharist.[34] Looking back, it was fairly cool towards the celebration of his presence in the Word. Fascinated by the "Blessed Sacrament"—as if the other sacraments were not holy, and as if the Word were not either!—it

---

[31] Acts 13:14-15.

[32] In the account of the Transfiguration, Moses and Elijah speak of the "exodus" of Jesus, Luke 9:31. On the links between the account of the Exodus and the life of Jesus, see J. Guillet, *Biblical Themes*, 9–25.

[33] John 4:34.

[34] See J.-C. Didier, *Histoire de la présence réelle*, coll. "Esprit et Vie," edt. CLD, 1978. [English parallel would be N. Mitchell, *Cult and Controversy*, Pueblo, 1982 on Berengarius.]

expressed itself above all in what one might well call a Eucharistic "totalitarianism": outside of the Mass and the worship of the most holy Sacrament, Catholics knew how to do little else. It is never a healthy state of affairs when a theology defines itself in reaction to theological discussions. One cannot build a peaceful house where truth dwells harmoniously if one builds in the shadow of polemics.

In the face of Eucharistic totalitarianism, Protestant theology insisted strongly on the presence of Christ in his Word and made *sola scriptura* (Scripture alone) the flag of its own claims. Sometimes, it even forgot the precept of the Lord, "Do this in memorial of me," and it neglected to celebrate the meal of the New Covenant.

This position was no better than the Catholic position, for it is just as true that a Protestant theology which defines itself in opposition to Catholic theology cannot attain a harmonious, balanced understanding of Christian faith.

Lastly, Catholics and Protestants may congratulate each other, for the little importance both have attributed to the third mode of Christ's presence: his presence at the heart of the celebrating community.

In reality, these three modes of the Risen Christ's presence—in the community, in the Word, and in the Eucharist—interpenetrate each other in a dynamic interrelation, forming together the full richness of the mystery which the Church celebrates.[35] In other words, an authentic celebration of the real presence of Christ is only properly achieved if it balances these three modes of real presence: in the community, in the Word, and in the Eucharist.

Of these three modes of presence, the presence of Christ in the celebrating community is primary. It is not because the community would be orphan children of Christ that it celebrates the Eucharist, as if to make an absent Christ present for its adoration. Rather, it is because Christ is already present in the community through its faith and love that the Church is capable of also rendering him present under the symbols of the Eucharistic bread and wine, and of celebrating the Covenant meal. One may also say that it is not to receive a Christ who no longer lives in them that the faithful receive him in Communion; rather it is because Christ is already present in them by faith and love that it is also fitting to receive him in the Eucharistic bread.

[35] Cf. L. Deiss, *The Supper of the Lord.*

Likewise, it is not because the community would otherwise be Christ's orphans that it celebrates the Word to render him present under the symbol of the inspired words. Rather it is because Christ dwells with his Church until the end of time[36] that the Church is capable of opening its heart to the Gospel addressed to it.

It has been said that the Church makes Eucharist and that the Eucharist makes the Church.[37] One may also affirm that the Church "creates" the Word, calling it into existence by its celebration (otherwise the Gospels remain only a library book), and inversely, that the Word creates the ecclesial community.

RELATION BETWEEN WORD AND EUCHARIST

The Word of God is of the same importance as the Eucharist.

We must now take a last step and ask: Is there a relation between the Word and the Eucharist? If so, what is this relation? In other words, is it a question of two mysteries which are simply juxtaposed—as in the past one referred to the ante-Mass and the Mass—or does an organic relationship link the two in the unity of a single mystery?

Vatican II opened a path of reflection:

> The two parts which in some way constitute the Mass, the liturgy of the Word and the Eucharistic liturgy, are so closely united that they form a single act of worship.[38]

The Council thus distinguished well the two parts—liturgy of the Word and the Eucharistic liturgy—which form the Mass. Yet it immediately united them both in the unity of a single act of worship.

What is this single act of worship?

The Mass is the celebration of the new Covenant. "This is the blood of the new Covenant" says the priest at Mass, taking up the words of Jesus at the Last Supper. These words refer directly to the Sinai Covenant: "This is the blood of the Covenant which Yahweh has made with you" says Moses on Sinai.[39]

[36] Matt 28:20.
[37] Cf. H. De Lubac, *Méditation sur L'Église*, Aubier. Paris, 1953, 115–117.
[38] *Sacrosanctum Concilium*, 56.
[39] Exod 24:8; Matt 26:28.

In the celebration of the Sinai Covenant, the Word is not only constitutive of the Covenant, it is the foundation upon which the Covenant is built.[40] The Word plays the same foundational role in the new Covenant which is celebrated in the Eucharist.

The feast of the Covenant at Sinai

Before writing its history in the books of the Bible, Israel lived it, then celebrated it, and finally projected onto the ancient biblical texts the experience of its cultic life. Thus the texts represent less the concrete historical outworking of the events of Israel's history than the ideal vision of their outworking conceived by Israel's faith, and then transmitted to each generation. This is particularly true for the most venerable texts, such as the account of the Sinai Covenant.

This account may be found in Exodus 24:1-11. It clearly brings together two sources of diverse origin:[41] The first is made up of verses 1a and 9-11. Here, the Covenant is sealed on the mountain by a communion meal. The second is made up of verses 3-8. Here, the Covenant is sealed at the foot of the mountain by a Covenant sacrifice. This is the text (the second source is the indented text):

He said to Moses: Come up toward Yahweh, you, Aaron, Nadab, Abihu and seventy elders of Israel. (You shall prostrate yourselves at a distance. Moses alone will approach Yahweh. They shall not approach, and the people shall not come up with him.)

> Moses came to tell to the people all the words of Yahweh and all the rules. All the people replied with a single voice: "All the words which Yahweh has said, we will put into practice."

---

[40] For the idea of the Covenant, see A. Jaubert, *La notion d'Alliance dans le Judaïsme*, Éditions du Seuil, 1963. L. Krinetzki, *Der Bund Gottes mit den Menschen nach dem Alten und Neuen Testament*, Patmos Verlag, Düsseldorf, 1964. D. J. McCarthy, *Old Testament Covenant*, Blackwell, Oxford, 1973 (with bibliography, 90–108). P. Buis, *La notion D'Alliance dans l'Ancien Testament*, coll. "Lectio Divina, Cerf, Paris, 1976.

[41] It is not possible to attribute the texts with certitude to a yahwistic or an elohistic source. M. Noth (*Uperlieferungsgeschichte des Pentateuch*, Kohlhammer, Verlag, Stuttgart, 1948, 33) thinks that vv. 3-8 may represent a secondary addition, while R. De Vaux (*Histoire ancienne d'Israel*, coll. "Études Bibliques," J. Gabalda, Paris, 1971, 415) prefers to attribute them to an elohistic source. Cf. D. Doré, "Un repas 'd'alliance'? Exod 24:1-2, 9-11," *Le Point Théologique*, 24 (1977) 147–170, with bibliographical note, 170–171.

Moses wrote all the words of Yahweh. He got up very early in the morning, he built an altar at the foot of the mountain, with twelve steles for the twelve tribes of Israel.

Then he commissioned young Israelites to offer holocausts and to immolate before Yahweh young bulls as communion sacrifices. Moses took half the blood and put it in basins, and he sprinkled the altar with the other half.

He took the book of the Covenant and he read it in the hearing of the people, who declared: "All that Yahweh had said, we will put into practice and we will obey."

Moses took the blood, and sprinkling the people he said: "This is the blood of the Covenant which the Lord has made with you according to all these words."

Moses ascended, accompanied by Aaron, Nadab, Ahibu and the seventy elders of Israel. They contemplated the God of Israel. Under his feet saphires stretched out like a pavement, by their purity like heaven itself. He did not raise his hand against the notables of the children of Israel, and they were able to contemplate God. They ate and they drank.

In the *first account* (Exod 24:1a, 9-11), which is without doubt very ancient, Moses goes up the mountain to the Lord. He is accompanied by Aaron, Nadab and Ahibu (whom the later priestly tradition will identify with the sons of Aaron, Lev 10:1), as well as the seventy elders. These last are very important: they represent the whole of the people of Israel (cf. Num 11:16): the Covenant is concluded in the name of the entire people. "They ate and they drank" (v. 11). It is a Covenant meal.[42] What a marvel! Welcomed right to the door of heaven, Moses and his friends, having escaped from the Egyptian servitude, become the guests of God and eat at his table. "They contemplated the God of Israel" (v. 10): the statement is extraordinary. Entrance into the Covenant is—like faith—the beginning of a certain contemplation of the splendor of God!

The *second account* (Exod 24:3-8) focusses on the rite of sacrifice. The aspersion of the altar and the people signifies the union of the Lord and his community in the blood of the Covenant. God and the people become consanguine; they form a single family and share the same life (the blood is the sign of life, Lev 17:14). As in

[42] R. De Vaux, *op cit.*, 414: "The meal is the culminating point of the account and it must be regarded as a Covenant meal."

the Book of Joshua, the twelve pillars represent the twelve tribes of Israel and are witnesses to the Covenant.

The tradition of Israel did not read the two sources separately as we do today through our desire to approach the text analytically. Its faith received them as a single account of the feast of the Covenant.[43] In the celebration, the Word is organically linked to the Covenant:

> • Moses brings all the words of Yahweh and all the laws to the people (v. 3). He writes them in the book of the Covenant (v. 4), and he reads them to the people (v. 7).
> • The people, for their part, receive the Word, not simply listening passively, but entering actively into the plan of God. They commit themselves to be obedient: "All the words which Yahweh has said we will put into practice and obey" (v. 3, 7).
> • Lastly, the sacrificial rite which seals the union of God and his own is built upon the Word of God: "This is the blood of the Covenant which Yahweh has concluded with you, *according to all these words*" (v. 8).[44] The Word is thus constitutive of the Covenant, it is the base upon which the union of God and his people rests.

"The Covenant is inseparable from the Law . . . . The Law is the expression of the Covenant, according to the adage: The Covenant is the Law."[45]

The feasts of the Covenant

The Covenant is definitive. God will never take back his word. But the word of human beings is fragile. Their fidelity is fragile. The people of Sinai had scarcely finished promising: "All the words that Yahweh has said, we will put into practice" (Exod 24:3), before they began, only forty days later, to dance before the golden calf![46]

---

[43] D. Doré: "It is only in terms of a global reading of chapter 24 of Exodus that one may speak of a "Covenant rite." (cf. ref. note 41).

[44] The mention of *all these words* (v. 3) makes one recall Exod 20:1: "God pronounced *all these words*" which prefaces the Decalogue. *All these laws* makes one recall the Covenant Code (Exod 20:22–23:23) which is inserted between the Decalogue and Exod 24:1.

[45] R. Marin-Achard, *Essai sur les fêtes d'Israel*, Éditions Labor et Fides, Geneva, 1974, 68.

[46] Exod 24:3; 32:1-6.

It was therefore necessary to remind the people unceasingly of the exigencies of the Covenant. When the prophets pleaded "Remember Lord, do not break the Covenant that you have made with us!" (Jer 14:21), they knew well that Yahweh had a good memory, but they wanted above all to refresh the memory of the people.

It was also necessary to renew the Covenant when it had been manifestly broken by sin, for betrayal was part, alas, of Israel's path. Was not the sacred history of the chosen people first of all a history of the divine mercy which forgave unceasingly?

Lastly, subsequent generations had to be introduced into the Covenant, generations who, in every age, came to join themselves to the people born at Sinai, and to make with them the pilgrimage of love towards eternity.

It was to respond to these necessities that the feasts of the Covenant were celebrated.

The Deuteronomist introduced a sort of celebration of the Word every seven years. This frequency could vary no doubt according to the sanctuaries and epochs:

> Every seven years, at the times fixed for the year of remittance, during the feast of Tabernacles, at the moment when all Israel will come to see the face of Yahweh your God, in the place which he will have chosen, you shall read this Law in the hearing of all Israel (Deut 31:10-11).

Certain exceptional feasts of the Covenant renewal have marked the history of Israel at decisive moments—sometimes dramatic and are written in its flesh as indelible scars. There are the renewal of the Covenant after the episode of the golden calf, the celebration of Shichem after the entry into the promised land, the renewal of the Covenant during Ezekiel's reform, in about 716, and during Josiah's reform in 622.[47] These feasts allow us to gain a probable

---

[47] Exod 34:10; Jos 24 (cf. 8:30-35); 2 Chr 29:10; 2 Kgs 23:1-31. Cf. our *Vivre la Parole en communauté*, Desclée de Brouwer, 1974, 23–100.

One could add certain psalms that M. Manatti classifies among the Covenant Ritual psalms, for example, Ps 50 (*Les Psaumes*, vol. 1, Desclee de Brouwer, 1966, 41–46). However this type of psalm is not classified in S. Mowinckel, *The Psalms in Israel's Worship* (Blackwell, Oxford, 1962), nor in G. Castellino, *Libro dei Salmi* (Torino, Roma, Marietti, 1955), nor in A. Weiser, *Die Psalmen* (Vandenhoeck & Ruprecht, Gottingen, 7th ed., 1966) nor in H. Gunkel, *Die Psalmen* (5th ed., 7th ed., 1968), nor in H. J. Kraus, *Psalmen*, vol. 1 (Neukirchener Verlag, 1960), XXXVII–LVI. It is freely admitted however, that the context of a good number of the psalms may be cultic (cf.

idea of the ordinary feasts of the Covenant. They are:[48]

The convocation of "all Israel"

Psalm 50:5 has conserved an echo of this convocation:

> Assemble before me all my own,
> Those who sealed my Covenant by sacrifice.[49]

This convocation builds the Church (ek-klesia), community of those who are called (kletoi) out from the midst (ek) of the nations by the Word of God.

Celebration of the Word of God

The preaching of the Word of God, the heart of the celebration was made up of:

- The proclamation of the deed of Covenant. At Sinai, Moses "took the book of the Covenant and read it to the people." At Shichem, Joshua "read all the words of the Law—the blessings and the curses—according to all that was written in the book of the Law."[50]
- The homily, that is to say the explanation and the actualization of the Covenant. At Shichem, Joshua summoned the people to choose between Yahweh and strange gods—"Choose today whom you wish to serve"—and he implored them: "Put away strange gods from among your midst and incline your heart towards Yahweh, God of Israel."[51]
- The response of the assembly: the assembly accepts the plan of God. At Sinai the people cry out: "All the words that Yahweh has said, we will put into practice." And at Shichem: "We wish to serve Yahweh; he is our God."[52]

A. Descamps, "Les genres littéraires du Psautier'" in R. De Langhe, *Le Psautier*, coll. "Orientalia et Biblica Lovaniensia," IV, Louvain, 1962, 80–85; A. Weiser, *op cit.*, 23), and that the *Sitz im Leben* of certain psalms may be the Covenant cult (*Bundeskult*).

[48] Cf. P. Buis, *La notion d'Alliance, op. cit.*, 159.

[49] Cf. H. J. Kraus, *Psalmen* for the links between Ps 50 and the celebration of the Covenant, 372–376.

[50] Exod 24:7; Josh 8:34. Sometimes Yahweh is moved to speak himself to the people (Exod 24:10-11; Josh 24:2).

[51] Josh 24:15, 23.

[52] Exod 24:3; Josh 24:34. P. Buis adds the proclamation of blessings and curses to this ritual, which play the role of an oath, and that the people ratify by their Amen (Josh 8:24; Deut 28).

Sacrificial rite or communion sacrifice

These rites signify the union of God and the people. At Sinai the sacrificial rite is underlined by the words of Moses who sprinkles the assembly with the blood of the victims and says:

"This is the blood of the Covenant which Yahweh has concluded with you." As for the communion meal, the text says superbly: "The seventy elders contemplated the God of Israel . . . they ate and they drank."[53]

Whatever the flexibility of the rites and the diversity of historical situations, there is always an essential element in the celebrations of the Covenant that beats like a heart at the center of the rite, an element towards which all the affirmations of the biblical sources tend. This element may be summarized thus: "Listen, Israel!"

The Sinai Covenant, while being a totally unique and irreversible event found once and for all in the web of history, is at the same time, a "foundational" (*Urversammlung*[54]) assembly to which all the later assemblies come to draw their existence. It is the master link that holds together all the other links and gives consistency to the bond of love that links God to the people. The Covenant, sealed once and for all with the people at Sinai, is concluded with Israel throughout the ages. At each celebration the refrain is heard again: "This is the Covenant which Yahweh has made with you, according to all these words." Throughout its history, Israel verified the adage: "The Covenant is the Law."

The Eucharistic celebration, feast of the new Covenant

The Mass is the celebration of the Covenant.[55] Taking up the words of Moses at Sinai, Jesus affirmed at the Last Supper: "This is the blood of the Covenant," and this Covenant is spoken of as "new."[56] These are the same words that the priest says at Mass.

[53] Exod 24:8, 9, 11. In the rite of Covenant renewal by Ezechiel (2 Chr 29:10), one finds both an expiatory sacrifice (vv. 21-24) and a communion sacrifice (vv. 31-36).

[54] A. Arens (*Die Psalmen im Gottesdienst des Alten Bundes*, Paulinus-Verlag, Trier, 1961, 27) writes: "Each renewal of the Covenant forms an internal unity with the original assembly" (*Urversammlung*).

[55] Matt 26:28.

[56] Luke 22:20; 1 Cor 11:25.

The Mass reproduces exactly the scheme of the celebration on Sinai following the tradition handed down to us. It consists of both the celebration of the Word and the sacrifice of Communion in the Eucharistic liturgy. Vatican II speaks of "the two parts which constitute the Mass; the liturgy of the Word and the Eucharistic liturgy."[57]

Celebration of the Word

This Word proclaimed at Mass is a Covenant Word. It may be considered as an echo of the Word that Moses proclaimed on Sinai, or as a reflection of the preaching of the Covenant in the later celebrations which reflected the history of the chosen people, or lastly, as the continuation of the Good News which Jesus revealed to the world before he sealed the New Covenant in the sacrifice of the Cross.

Certainly the Word proclaimed at Mass is divided into multiple pericopes. Yet each fragment sends one back to the totality of revelation. Each pericope is a symbol of the whole. Each iota of the Law is precious to the degree that whoever observes it is supposed to observe all the Law, and, as Jesus said, "will be taken for great in the kingdom of heaven."[58] The Lectionary of the Mass becomes here the equivalent of "Book of the Covenant" that Moses proclaimed on Sinai. God seals the new Covenant with the people "according to all these words."

Celebration of the Eucharist

The Covenant celebrated in the Eucharist is called "new" precisely in regard to the Covenant of Sinai.[59] It is the prolongation of this Covenant and the prolongation of the other Covenant celebrations that mark the history of Israel en route towards Jesus. It also re-actualizes the sacrifice where Jesus, "mediator of a new Covenant,"[60] assumes by his death all the ancient sacrifices. Lastly, it re-actualizes all the communion sacrifices. The sublime scene where all the elders of Israel ascended the mountain of Sinai, con-

---

[57] *Sacrosanctum Concilium*, 56.
[58] Matt 5:19-20.
[59] According to Jer 31:32.
[60] Heb 9:15.

templated the God of glory, and ate and drank in his presence,[61] was a prophecy of the Eucharistic Communion in the Mass.

Link between Word and Eucharist

The link between Word and Covenant in the celebration on Sinai and in the later celebrations of the Covenant is the same link between Word and Eucharist in the celebration of the Mass. In other words, on Sinai as at Mass, the Word is the foundation of the Covenant. The new Covenant celebrated at Mass is concluded, like the ancient celebration on Sinai, "according to all these words." At each consecration, the priest, in the footsteps of Jesus, evokes the prophecy of the new Covenant according to Jeremiah: "I will put my Law in the depths of their being and I shall write it on their heart."[62]

When Vatican II speaks of "two parts that in some way constitute the Mass, the liturgy of the Word and the Eucharistic liturgy that are so closely united that they constitute a single act of worship,"[63] we must now understand that this single act of worship is the celebration of the new Covenant both in the Word that is proclaimed and in the bread and wine that are consecrated.

PASTORAL EXIGENCIES

These conclusions place a profound need for truth and authenticity at the heart of our celebrations. But this need, if one responds to it, is a source of joy and of peace. For nothing is more refreshing than a celebration where each element, fulfilling its ministerial function, promotes the joy of a living liturgy.

No celebration of the Eucharist without a real celebration of the Word

The Word proclaimed at Mass is the foundation of the Eucharist, sacrament of the new Covenant.

There must never be a celebration of the Eucharist without a real celebration of the Word. The community that is content simply to read the texts of the Word, has done nothing except to begin.

[61] Exod 24:9-11.
[62] Jer 33:33.
[63] *Sacrosanctum Concilium*, 56.

The community must welcome the Word in faith as a word of the Covenant, must commit itself to following the word as a response of love, must be ready to reply as did the community at Sinai: "All that Yahweh has said, we will put into practice and obey." Only then may the priest take the "cup of blessing" and say with Moses: "This is the blood of the Covenant that Yahweh has made with you according to all these words."

Formerly, one distinguished the ante-Mass which consisted of all the readings, and the Mass, properly speaking. The readings were supposed to be a preparation—as an hors-d'oeuvre—before the Eucharistic banquet. The barrier which separated the ante-Mass was placed just before the Offertory. Whoever succeeded in joining the Sunday flock before this barrier was reached, even if they missed all the readings, including the Gospel, was thought to have assisted at Mass, to have accomplished their Sunday duty, and thus to be saved for all eternity. If our conclusions are just, we must now say that the Mass, the celebration of the Covenant, begins with the first reading. Whoever misses a reading harms the integrity of the celebration of the Covenant. They tear apart the unity of the celebration, since, according to Vatican II, the liturgy of the Word and the liturgy of the Eucharist constitute a single act of worship. They attack the dignity of the Word of the Covenant and the dignity of the Eucharist which is built upon this Word.

The Council taught: "Christ is present in his Word, for he speaks whenever the holy Scriptures are read in the Church."[64] What member of the faithful could pretend that they adore Christ present in his Word when they neglect to adore him in this presence? Who could say that they venerate the presence of Christ in the community when they impoverish the community and wound it by showing so little eagerness to come together? Lastly, who could affirm that they desire to listen to the Word of their Lord and God when they forget, either through laziness or negligence, to be there when Jesus begins to speak?

This celebration of the Word may take diverse forms

In a monastic community, for example, it could be enough to add to the reading of the Word one or two phrases of homily and

---

[64] *Sacrosanctum Concilium*, 7.

to conclude with a brief prayer of the faithful. Familiar with interior meditation and the prayer of contemplation, the community does not have need of other aids and finds itself fully at ease with extended silence. In a catechumenal community, on the contrary—I am thinking concretely of certain African communities in mission countries—it is necessary to amplify the Word by giving it a joyful, living resonance. First one reads the Gospel in the translation called "official." Then the catechist—or someone who has the charism of the Word—recounts the Gospel again in their own way. They may embellish the Gospel text with a thousand splendors.

Sometimes, the text is mimed in order to understand it better. The celebration of the Word is cut up into multiple dialogues, songs, prayers, and dances. This manner of celebrating, where improvisation is queen, weds perfectly the tradition of these communities.

For our ordinary Western communities, the celebration may be simpler. The minimum to attain is that the celebrating community, at least in its heart, responds following the assembly at Sinai: "All that Jesus has said, we will obey and put into practice!" The homily which actualizes the Word, and the prayer of the faithful that responds to it with supplication, are the ordinary paths of this ideal.

For example, let us suppose that the Gospel is that of the Beatitudes: "Happy the poor of heart, for the kingdom of heaven is theirs." The minimum homily would be to say: "Today, Jesus invites us to the happiness of living according to his poverty. All that Jesus has said, we will obey and put into practice. Amen." And the minimum of prayer—whatever the literary form of this prayer— would reduce itself to "Lord Jesus, help us to put into practice all that you have said and to be happy by living according to your poverty. Amen.

Paul said in regard to the Eucharist: "Let each one examine themself."[65] This rule is equally applicable to the Word: let each community examine itself, so that it recognizes and does what is in conformity with the will of God.

Only the Word of God . . .

If the Word of God is the foundation of the Eucharist, it follows that only the Word of God may be used for the readings in the Eucharistic celebration.

[65] 1 Cor 11:28.

The document *Dominicae Cenae* explains this clearly:

> The reading of Scripture may not be replaced by the reading of other texts, even those possessing an undeniable religious and moral value. On the contrary, these texts may be used with great profit in the homily. The homily lends itself very well in fact to the utilization of these texts . . . for it belongs to the nature of the homily, among other things, to show the convergences between divine wisdom and noble human thought which seeks the truth through diverse paths.[66]

All human words, however noble and worthy, may illustrate the Word of God. But no human word can replace the Word of God.

The grace of a certain length in the celebration

In order to celebrate the Word fittingly, the grace of a certain length of celebration is necessary. Formerly, the low Tridentine Mass lasted about half an hour. Today, the "new" Mass may be "executed"—this word is apt—in twenty minutes, sometimes less. The Eastern Orthodox tradition, which honors the mysteries by celebrating them with a wise sedateness and a holy fullness,[67] is scandalized at the precipitation which we sometimes exhibit in our Latin rite. Mgr. Elias Zoghby, Catholic archbishop of Baalbeck, said: "The 'Catholic' liturgy is, apart from on certain feast days and in certain convents and cathedrals, reduced to a 'Mass-making machine' and to an isolated Eucharistic sacrifice, detached, or almost, from the divine Office."[68] This judgement of a Catholic bishop, whose sensibility has remained so close to that of Orthodox spirituality, may appear severe. It calls for an explanation from our communities.

A calm and joyous celebration of the Word must make us forget forever the Catholic image of the "Mass-making machine" and lead each community to the "grace of a certain length."

If one counts the time of the homily and of the prayer of the faithful, if one adds the spaces of silence which are recommended in the penitential rite, before the opening prayer, after the homily

---

[66] *Dominicae Coenae* (24 February 1980) 10. Cf. also *Inaestimabile Donum* (3 April 1980).

[67] The Eucharistic celebration may easily last between two and three hours. However, it is not celebrated every day.

[68] In *Tous schismatiques?*, Beirut, 1981, 137–138.

and the prayer of the faithful, and the time of personal thanksgiving after Communion, one should obtain a peaceful rhythm in which the community can move to encounter its God.

We may ask ourselves if our Christian communities with their priests are capable of evolving on this point. Certain habits, which have taken on the mask of tradition, are worse than prisons.

No celebration of the Word without celebration of the Covenant

Our first conclusion was: "No celebration of the Eucharist without celebration of the Word." This conclusion must be complemented by the following: "No celebration of the Word without a celebration of the Covenant."

Word and Spiritual Communion

If Word and Covenant are inseparable, the grace of the celebration of the Word is thus the grace of the Covenant. At Mass, this grace of the Covenant is signified especially by sacramental Communion. If the ideal of participation in the Mass is: no Mass without Communion, we may also affirm: no celebration of the Word without spiritual Communion. It is towards the spiritual grace of the Eucharist that the whole celebration of the Word tends, towards what we call spiritual Communion.

Word and Sacramental Communion

This reality of grace relativizes somewhat the problem of sacramental Communion in the Sunday assemblies (or others) which are celebrated in the absence of a priest, but which have the possibility of including the distribution of the reserved sacrament. Must one conclude every celebration of the Word with a distribution of Communion?[69]

There is no direct advantage in integrating Communion in such a celebration. And there is no direct advantage in excluding it. The important thing is not the rite of Communion but the grace of the sacrament. This grace of union with God is precisely what the

---

[69] The *Directory for Sunday Assemblies in the Absence of a Priest* (Congregation for Divine Worship, 2 June 1988) 28, recommends the distribution of Communion.

celebration of the Word aims to attain in so far as it is the foundation of the Covenant. What is important is not whether to receive Communion or not, but to enter into the Covenant with God. One may conceive then of celebrations of the Word without sacramental Communion, the assembly having been prepared for Covenant commitment by the Word. One may also conceive of such celebrations with Communion, the sacrament ratifying the grace created by the Word.

What counts is not first of all the sacramental reception of the bread and wine in the Eucharist, but the relation of faith and love which unites each member of the faithful to Christ Jesus.

Word and daily Eucharist

The value accorded to the celebration of the Word can illumine our understanding of the Eastern Churches. In the majority of these rites, as we know, priests do not celebrate the Eucharist daily. The Patriarch Athenagoras, of holy memory, only celebrated the Eucharist seven times each year, "according to the rules of the Church of Constantinople."[70] In the Roman rite, on the contrary, Vatican II recommends that priests celebrate daily Mass.[71] What may one think of the diversity of these usages?

Neither the Roman rite nor the Eastern rites may pretend to reflect an ancient tradition that would be normative.[72] The practice of Churches has varied in the course of history as well as within the same rite. To pretend that the practice recommended by Vatican II to priests of the Roman rite is better than the practice of the Eastern Churches is quite simply false. The Roman practice is simply different from the practice of the other rites.

That having been said, the wandering demons of rubricism prowl around in the ritual pathways of the Roman Mass, just as in the Eastern liturgies. The best practice, for the Roman rite as for the Eastern rites, is that which seeks with the greatest truth, beyond all rubrics, the very grace of the Covenant, whether in the daily celebration of the Word or in the daily celebration of the Eucharist.

[70] O. Clement, *Dialogue avec le Patriarche Athénagoras*, edt. Fayard, Paris, 1969, 111.

[71] *Presbyterorum Ordinis*, 13.

[72] See R. Taft, "The Frequency of the Eucharist through History," in *Concilium*, 172, February 1982, 27–44.

Word and Liturgy of the Hours

A last word on the "Liturgy of the Hours." Each celebration includes regularly a "brief reading" of the Word of God. Most of the time and in most communities, one is content to read the text with devotion. There is then a moment of silence. Then the celebration continues. Word proclaimed, rubric executed, conscience appeased . . . . We have already cited this "rule."

Is this all there is to the celebration?

It is evident that Christians are not baptized in order to read readings, nor to celebrate the Liturgy of the Hours or the Mass, but rather to encounter the God of the Covenant. The celebration of the Word is the path of this grace.

The *General Instruction on the Liturgy of the Hours* makes a timid appeal for a celebration of the Word when it proposes:

> When the celebration is carried out in the presence of the faithful, one may add, when it seems indicated, a brief homily in order to make the reading better understood.[73]

One may also make the Word of God resound in the hearts of the faithful by representing it in song. Music helps to memorize the Word and makes it return unceasingly to the surface of the heart. How long the path which must lead each community, from a reading of the Word, even when a short homily or song is added, to the celebration of the grace of the Covenant!

[73] *Institutio generalis de Liturgia Horarum*, 15 March 1971.

3
The Responsorial Psalm

The Responsorial Psalm "is an integral part of the Liturgy of the Word."[1] Because of this, Augustine liked to take it as the basis of his homily.[2] Tradition places it normally after the Old Testament readings,[3] as an intercalary chant.

In the pre-Vatican II Mass, this psalm, called the Gradual, had been reduced to an organ-witness: only two verses remained. The Word of God was drowned by the wanderings of Gregorian neumes. Sometimes, what musical splendor! Even the most beautiful compositions of the Gregorian repertoire were found here. But the restoration of the Word of God necessitated the restoration of the Responsorial Psalm. There was no choice. It was either the delights of the *jubilus*[4] and its lesser offspring—ephemeral, like all human beauty!—or the Word of God and its eternity.

What were the stakes of this reform? The stakes, which were immense, were the following: in his last appearance to his disciples, according to the testimony of Luke, the risen Christ spoke of what had been written of him "in the Law of Moses, in the Prophets and in the Psalms."[5] Thus we see the importance of the Responsorial

---

[1] See *GIRM*, 36.

[2] See *Enarrationes in Psalmos*, completed about 416.

[3] Thus they did in the churches of Syria in about 380, according to the witness of the *Apostolic Constitutions*, II, 57 (see M. Metzger, *Les Constitutions Apostoliques*, SC, 320 (1985), 54–62.

[4] On the *jubilus*, see 173.

[5] Luke 24:44.

Psalm: it is a question of restoring the face of Christ, as it appears in the psalms for the benefit of the Christian community. Certainly the faithful are supposed to know the psalter by other means. They are even warmly invited to participate in the Liturgy of the Hours,[6] in which the prayer of the psalms is the essential component. This participation has remained an unrealized ideal. In practice, each Sunday's Responsorial Psalm is their only contact with the psalter. Just as the Sunday Lectionary is their Bible, so the Responsorial Psalm is their psalter. Thus we see the importance of the reform of the Responsorial Psalm.

MINISTERIAL FUNCTION

A response to the Word of God

The Responsorial Psalm may be considered as the *response* of the community to the Word that is given to it.[7] Certainly, it is clear that the essential response is obedience to God and adoration of God's holy will. The Responsorial Psalm ritualizes this response.

The history of Israel is a continual dialogue with God. God speaks to the people in creating marvels for them. The people respond in blessing the God who does marvels. The acclamation of the psalm:

> Blessed be the Lord who works for us
> the marvels of his love![8]

reveals the heart of Israel and shows perfectly her response to God.

When the divine intervention is particularly decisive, the response of the community takes the form of a biblical canticle. Thus during the period of the Judges, when Yahweh delivers Israel from twenty years of oppression, Deborah and Barak sing to the liberating God who, in the twinkling of the stars and in the bubbling

---

[6] *Institutio generalis de Liturgia Horarum* (15 March 1971), 20, 21, 26, and especially 33, 270.

[7] The Responsorial Psalm "is normally chosen in relation to the reading which precedes it."

[8] Ps 31:22. We take up again certain elements looked at in *Notitiae* 24, 1966, 365–372 and in *La Maison-Dieu*, 166, 1986, 61–82, elements which based themselves on our study *God's Word and God's People*, Collegeville, The Liturgical Press, 1976.

of the sacred stream of Kishon, destroys the enemy. God delivers
Anne from her sterility; Anne sings to the savior God, who makes
the sterile give birth seven times. God lets the people of the Exodus
pass through the Red Sea; Miriam praises the Lord with the tam-
bourine, the Lord who shows forth his glory and who throws horse
and rider into the sea.[9] And in the New Testament God accomplishes
the ancient promises made to Abraham by giving Jesus; Mary glori-
fies the Lord, she exults for joy in God her Savior, in this Jesus whom
she bears in her womb. God frees Zechariah from his muteness and
reveals that with the birth of John the Baptist the dawn of messianic praise has arrived. Zechariah blesses the God of Israel, the
rising Sun which shines upon the darkness of the world. God lets
Simeon hold the tiny child Jesus in his arms, the light of the nations and the glory of Israel. Simeon blesses God and sings his
praise.[10]

The reading of the Word of God in the liturgical celebration is
not simply the reading of the archives of the people of God of the
Old and New Testament, but the actualization ("Today this Word
is accomplished"[11]) for the benefit of the celebrating community of
the events of the prophecies about which the Word speaks. The community responds to this actualization of the Word in the liturgical
celebration by actualizing its praise in the Responsorial Psalm. One
may make the following parallel: just as in the history of the chosen people the community responds to God's marvels by the biblical canticle, so the liturgical community responds to the Word—
which actualizes for it these marvels—by the Responsorial Psalm.

A meditative chant?

The Responsorial Psalm is sometimes presented as a "meditative chant." This title is unknown in the tradition.[12] It is witness
to the epoch where the Gradual had become the prey of the vocal
virtuosity of the psalmist or of the schola: the people, having no
longer anything to do during this time, were invited to meditate.

[9] Judg 5:2-31; 1 Sam 2:1-10; Exod 15:1-21.
[10] Luke 1:46-47, 67-68; 2:28-32.
[11] Luke 4:21.
[12] R. Cabie. The Church at Prayer, vol. II. Collegeville: The Liturgical Press, 1986.

In itself, the invitation to meditate on the Word of God is always opportune.[13] The psalmist sang:

How I love your law!
All the day long, I meditate on it.[14]

Yet the problem is not there. The real question is the following: is it right to treat the Responsorial Psalm as a meditation chant, and thus to favor, by the magic of music, a climate of recollection and meditation? No. At least, not necessarily.

A quick reflection can provide an element of response. When the Responsorial Psalm proclaims: "All you people, clap your hands," or "Exult in the Lord! Dance before his face," or "Let us bow, let us prostrate ourselves. Let us kneel before the God who made us,"[15] one readily understands that the celebrating community is not being called to recollect itself in meditation, but simply to clap its hands, to dance for God, to prostrate itself before God. Certainly, one may meditate while dancing. But neither the dance nor the clapping of hands are the normal paths of meditation.

If one takes time to stand back, one may also affirm that the psalter collects together compositions the redaction of which has taken place over about a thousand years and which has been put together according to varied literary genres.[16] One finds *liturgies* (such as the lucernarium in Ps 134) *hymns* (such as the triumphant litany of the great hallel (Ps 136), *kingship psalms* in which the acclamation "God reigns" triumphs (such as Pss 96–100), the *royal psalms* centered on the Davidic monarchy (such as Ps 2), *lamentations, wisdom psalms*, and *historical psalms, canticles of Zion* and *prophetic exhortations*. Also there are *supplications* and individual and collective *thanksgivings* in the psalter. Without doubt, it

---

[13] *OLM* 22: "If one does not sing the psalm that follows the first reading, one should read it in a manner that favors meditation on the Word of God."

[14] Ps 119:97.

[15] Ps 47:2; 68:9; 95:7.

[16] Certain psalmic fragments, such as those of Ps 18:29-68, may go back to the period of the Judges, to the eleventh or even the twelfth century B.C. The most ancient psalm could be Ps 29 (see H.-J. Kraus, *Psalmen*, coll. Biblischer Kommentar, Altes Testament, XV/l, vol. 1, Neukirchener Verlag, 1960, LVIII. The compilation of the Pslater was completed at the latest by the middle of the second century B.C. (O. Eissfeldt, *Einleitung in das Alte Testament*, J.C.B. Mohr, Tübingen, third ed., 1964, 608). On the literary genres, see M. Manatti, *op. cit.*, 41–74. L. Sabourin, *Un classement littéraire des Psaumes*, Desclée de Brouwer, 1964.

is not possible to categorize perfectly all the psalms, there are intermediate genres: the frontier which separates a thanksgiving psalm from a prayer of trust may be permeable. Yet, it is impossible to confuse a lamentation with a hymn or an historical psalm with a canticle of Zion.

In plunging one's hand into the treasury of the psalter in order to pull out a text for the Responsorial Psalm, one necessarily pulls out a psalm marked by its literary genre. If the psalm is a lamentation, the Responsorial Psalm will be a lamentation. If it is a thanksgiving, the Responsorial Psalm will be a thanksgiving. If an historical psalm, it will be an historical account. And if it is a meditation on the Word—as is the case in Psalm 119—it will be a meditation. Thus meditation is not therefore excluded, but one may not reduce the Responsorial Psalm to a meditative chant.

EXECUTION OF THE RESPONSORIAL PSALM

Let us mention, simply to remind ourselves, of the two ways in which the Responsorial Psalm may be executed according to the *Ordo Lectionum* (n. 20). The first way is the *responsorial* form: the psalmist reads or sings the verses of the psalm, the assembly intervenes with a response (a refrain or an antiphon). The *Ordo* privileges this form: "It is to be preferred in so far as this is possible." The second way is the *direct* form: the psalm is read or sung straight through by the psalmist or by the assembly, without any interventions.

One may legitimately suppose that the Christian community has not yet exploited all the possible ways of executing the Responsorial Psalm. The *Ordo* (n. 21) recommends besides that "every means available in the various cultures is to be employed."

Here are some reflections:

To sing or to read?

In the biblical traditon, the psalter is called *tehillim*, (book of) *praises*, or *mizmorot*, (book of) *songs*. The Greek translates *psalmoi* as songs accompanied by the *psalterion*, the zither. We presume therefore that all the psalms were songs. The *Ordo Lectionem* (n.

20) presumes that the Responsorial Psalm is normally sung (*de more cantu proferatur*), which indicated implicitly that it may also be read. What is the ideal in practice?

The ideal is to respect the literary genre of each psalm. One must sing the songs and read the readings. This makes good sense. Therefore the psalms that are clearly songs, for example, the hymnic structured psalms, the kingship psalms, the canticles of Zion, and generally the thanksgiving psalms and the lamentations, should be sung. How can one not sing Psalm 96 which begins thus:

> Sing to the Lord a new song
> Sing to the Lord all the earth,
> Sing to the Lord and bless his name.

On the contrary, it seems fitting to read the psalms that are recitations, such as the historical psalms and the wisdom psalms.[17] When the "canticle" of Deuteronomy[18] reads: "Listen, O heaven, and I will speak," one wants to say: "Speak then, and we will listen."

Between these two extremes of an ornately structured song and a simple reading, there is a whole group of psalms which one may either sing, chant or read. The golden rule seems to be that which the *Ordo Lectionum* (n. 14) presents: "The singing should not weaken the power of the words but rather enhance them." Whenever singing does not help us to listen to the Word of God, it is better not to sing.

Solo singing of the psalm

The cantillation of readings or the chanting of psalms adds a festive note to the celebration. These may greatly enhance the effectiveness of the sacred texts.[19] S. Corbin writes: "The sung word has a mystical value. It is not an art in itself, nor present simply to decorate the worship, but is a sort of bridge between human beings and God."[20]

---

[17] It is also recommended in *Institutio generalis de Liturgia Horarum* (15 March 1971), 279.

[18] Deut 32:1.

[19] See L. Deiss, "La cantillation des lectures" in *Concile et chant nouveau, op. cit.* Levain, Paris, 1968, 245-258. The cantillation is a sung proclamation, in the manner of a chanting of the readings.

[20] *L'Église à la conquête de sa musique*, Gallimard, 1960, 61.

But solo cantillation, in which the soloists find themselves alone in front of the assembly, especially if they sing "without a net," that is, without the protection of the accompaniment of an organ, is a redoubtable task. Solo singing presupposes a voice good enough to make itself accepted by the whole community, and humble enough to allow itself to be forgiven by the community for singing in front of it. In those ministries where one finds oneself alone in front of the assembly, the human sympathy factor is of great importance.

If one decides to chant the psalm solo, it should be done with the greatest possible perfection. Solo chanting will not suffer any mediocrity. Certainly, it is not required that the soprano should have the voice of Elizabeth Schwartzkopf, nor the tenor, that of Dietrich Fischer-Dieskau. Besides, our communities require nothing of the sort. But one may ask of soloists that when they sing for God, they should make efforts comparable to those that these artists make when they sing for human beings.

Mercy for our soloists, we say! Agreed. But mercy also for the Word of God. And honor to all those who minister with humility for the joy and devotion of their sisters and brothers.

Word and Music

In the Responsorial Psalm, the Word of the psalm and the music of the psalm tone are in dialogue. One may lend one's ear more to either the message of the Word or the melody of the music. A certain tension may therefore be born according to whether one privileges listening to the Word or being captivated by the music.

An equilibrium must be found, but this equilibrium is not to be established between the Word and the music as if both have the same weight. The music is servant to the Word. The Word is queen. One comes from the earth. The other comes from heaven. How could it be possible to create an equilibrium between the ashes of human music and the gold of the divine Word? A true equilibrium demands that the music adore God present in his Word.

The music must lead the community to prayer.[21] The psalmody must be a path of contemplation. This cannot happen if the musician, that is, the psalmist, and all those who accompany the sing-

---

[21] *OLM*, 19, asks that the psalms be seen as a prayer of the Church.

ing, are not in a state of prayer. No one can direct the prayer of the community if they do not pray first of all themselves.

Let the music sing!

Servant of the Word of God, the music keeps its full dignity in this service. Let the servant thus sing![22] But let it respect the beauty of its mistress, the literary genre of each psalm.

The restoration of the Responsorial Psalm has brought forth in all the liturgies of the world numerous psalm tones. These tones have the immense advantage of encouraging the singing of all the psalms. They have the major inconvenience of reducing the singing of all the psalms to these same tones (as happened formerly when the Gregorian psalm tones were used to sing the psalms in Latin). To sing a kingship psalm—such as the triumphant acclamation "God reigns!"—such as the triumphant acclamation "God reigns!"—on a psalm tone groveling on three notes, or to sing a lamentation— such as the complaint—"By the waters of Babylon there we sat and wept"[23]—on a jubilant psalm tone, is the surest means of murdering the literary genres. In the end one risks anesthetizing the power of the Word.

The psalm tones are not like clothing that one may rent to clothe the psalms. In their extraordinary diversity, from the murmuring of imploration to cries of jubilation, the psalms possess an unimagined power. An anaemic psalm tone must not level all into a pious droning.

There is a lot of creative musical work to be done in this area.

TOWARDS THE FUTURE

With the restoration of the Responsorial Psalm, we have the psalter of the Christian community. Through it, the face of Christ Jesus, hidden for centuries under the beauty of Gregorian chant, appears again in its radiant splendor. Yet no reform is perfect. We may always dream of making it still better.

[22] "As a rule the responsorial psalm should be sung," *OLM* 20.
[23] Ps 137:1.

The Responsorial Psalm is chosen in reference to the readings. There is a *congruentia*, says the *Ordo Lectionum*,[24] a rapport between the psalm and the readings, especially the first reading. Thus the psalm is tailored to bring out the value of the readings. But the psalms have their own value, not only in their *congruentia* with other readings. It is not the psalter of the Bible which we have here, but that of the Lectionary. Certainly, it is normal to suppose that the psalms have been well chosen. Yet one may still dream of a liturgy where the psalm would be prayed, sung, celebrated, for its own value as Word of God, for the revelation it gives us of the mystery of Christ.

The Responsorial Psalm presents the psalm not in its entirety but ordinarily in three stanzas of four lines. Thus it is not an entire psalm but of a pericope of a psalm. This "cutting up" is not a major inconvenience when the original psalm does not have a literary structure, which is the case in psalmic compositions that are litanies, such as the interminable Psalm 119 on the Law of God. But when the psalm is constructed according to a solid literary structure—in the case of the hymns, for example, this sometimes resembles a mutilation. The Christian community that Sunday after Sunday prays the Responsorial Psalm will never know the admirable history of Psalm 103, nor that of the paschal Psalm 118, nor that of Psalm 138, where we sing with the angels: "Lord, your love endures forever!" It will only have a few weakened echoes of the tortures of the Passion and the glory of the Resurrection portrayed in Psalms 22 and 31, psalms which Christ prayed on the Cross when he said: "My God, my God, why have you abandoned me?" and "Into your hands I commit my spirit"!

One dreams of a community that would have the time to pray these prayers in their entirety, prayers which are at the heart of the piety of the Old Testament and also at the heart of the prayer of Jesus.

Some psalms have escaped this "cutting up." They are short: one must not "lengthen" the celebration of the Mass, but they are rare. For example, in Year A, there are only three: Psalms 23, 122, 131. If "lengthening" the celebrations by only a few seconds had been acceptable, one could have retained a number of other psalms.[25]

---

[24] *OLM*, 19. See also note 7 above.

[25] Of the whole of the Psalter, one could have retained the integrity of the following psalms: 4, 8, 15, 23, 43, 46, 47, 70, 86, 93, 100, 113–117, 120–131, 133, 134, 138,

One dreams of a community which would not be so miserly with its time.[26] Each psalm recounts a history with infinite dimensions. That of a prayer which rises towards the Father and is heard. Each psalm recounts the history of the prayer of Jesus. It is this prayer which we take up. "He prays for us, he prays in us, he is prayed to by us," explains St. Augustine.[27] "Let us recognize therefore our words in him and his words in us." Would Jesus thus shorten the psalms?

One hopes for communities that would possess the psalter—or at least a liturgical psalter—as they possess a book of song, and would with Jesus celebrate leisurely and fully the Father in heaven.

The psalter is "the book of song and prayer of the post-exilic community."[28] Nowhere is such prayer and song so spiritual. Yet nowhere is the body used in this spiritual celebration. Nowhere else in the Bible is there so much dancing, nowhere else does one prostrate oneself so often, nowhere else are so many festive processions organized. It is truly the whole human person, body and spirit that is taken up in a tornado of praise, adoration, and imploration. All this is accompanied by flutes, trumpets, harps, lyres, cymbals, tambourines, drums . . . ! These words of fire in which Israel cried her anguish, prostrated herself in ashes, sang of her ecstasy, leapt with joy, have become in the soothing sweetness of three chanted stanzas, a sluggish text, without light.

How many times shall we hear the psalmist at the ambo invite us to prostrate ourselves before God (Ps 95:6), to praise him by the dance (Ps 149:3), to lift up hands in intense prayer (Ps 63:5), to organize festive processions to the sound of the music and the rhythm of the tambourines shaken by young girls (Ps 68:26), and nothing happens, neither in the nave and still less in the sanctuary. We remain seated in our pews as though paralyzed, in an attitude

---

147, 148, and 150. This gives thirty-five psalms, which is more than 23 percent of the hundred and fifty psalms of the whole psalter, and more than 27 percent of the hundred and twenty-eight psalms of the Mass Lectionary (of Solemnities, the Sunday and festive cycle, the ritual and votive Masses and "Ad diversa").

[26] This problem of time is insoluble in parishes where Sunday Masses, because of the number of the faithful, follow immediately upon one another without interruption. The only solution would be to create smaller communities. But this is another problem.

[27] *Enarratio in Psalm*, 85:1, *CCL*, 39:1176. Cited in *Institutio generalis de Liturgia Horarum* 7, 15 March 1971.

[28] H.-J. Kraus, *Psalmen*, vol. 1, *op. cit.* 18.

of meditative compunction, without dreaming, even for an instant, to bow before God. Would it be contrary to the piety of the New Testament to acclaim the God of marvels with cries of joy, to celebrate God's love with the dance? Certainly, all this implies an interior attitude of heart. But in the prayer inspired by the Holy Spirit, one does not pray without one's body.

It is not a question of asking those communities who do not wish to do so to express themselves as the psalms suggest. But it is even less a question of forbidding those communities who wish to do so.

It is said in Psalm 68:4 that

> The just exult before the face of God,
> They dance with joy.

May we be those just!

CONCLUSION
THE CANTICLE OF THE COVENANT

The celebration of the Word, as we have seen, is the celebration of the Covenant. The Lectionary explains that "the community receives the Word of the Covenant . . . in order to become, day by day, ever more the people of the new Covenant."[29] The Responsorial Psalm, canticle of this Word, is the canticle of the Covenant. It prepares for the Covenant, it makes us enter the Covenant, it responds to the Word of the Covenant, it sings of its grace, it begs God to keep us within such grace. And this song of the Covenant is the very song which the Spirit of God invents.

A repertoire of a certain number of psalms which may have been utilized in the liturgy of the Old Testament for the celebration of the renewal of the Covenant has been drawn up. In using the Psalter in the liturgy for the renewal of the new Covenant at Mass, the whole psalter has been promoted to the dignity of a "ritual of the Covenant."

Just as one may not replace the Gospel by a simply human reading, however good it is, or as one may not replace the Eucharistic

[29] *OLM*, 45.

bread by ordinary bread, so too one should not think of replacing the Responsorial Psalm by an ordinary canticle. In each psalm it is the face of Christ himself which is revealed to the community: the face of the man of sorrows in the lamentations, the face of the Risen one in the kingship psalms, the face of the Master of wisdom in the wisdom psalms, the face of imploration in the psalms of supplication, and the face of praise and of blessing in the hymnic psalms. How dare we replace this adorable face whose traits have been drawn by the Holy Spirit by another face whose traits, fruit of human imagination, are drawn in a canticle?

Happy the communities who know how to discover in each psalm the face of the risen Christ! Happy those who pray with the psalm:

My heart repeats your word:
Seek my face!
It is your face O Lord that I seek (Ps 27:8).

The path travelled since Vatican II is a path of marvels. A much longer path, even more marvellous, remains to be travelled.

4
The Homily

INTRODUCTION

The word "homily" comes from the Greek *homilia*, which signifies reunion, assembly, company, familiar relations or conversa-
tion, discussion, exhortation. In religious vocabulary, "homily"
designates in a general manner a religious discourse. The word often
replaces "sermon," which is considered old-fashioned and worn out.

We understand "homily" here in its strict sense of a discourse
or exchange that explains and actualizes the Word of God.[1] Many
other sorts of discourse are possible in our assemblies: sermons,
eulogies, funeral orations. Sometimes these discourses are necessary on a pastoral level: it may be necessary to explain some con-
tested point of doctrine, to clarify some controversial point of
morality, to analyze some topical concern. We highly respect all
these types of discourse, and if a community likes this bread, we
must break such bread for its hunger. But we shall speak here of
the homily that responds to the supreme urgency: the explanation

---

[1] To designate the homily (biblical), the Latin tradition utilizes the words *tractatus* or *enarratio* (cf. Augustine, *Enarrationes in Psalmos* and the *Tractatus in Johan-
nem . . .* I). In the fourth century, the word *"sermon"* appears: it marks the decline
of the *lectio continua* of the Bible in liturgical assemblies. See J. Longère, *La prédication médiévale*, Études augustiniennes, Paris, 1983, 26–27, which gives precious in-
sights into the history of preaching (p. 19–138).

The *OLM* treats the homily in no 24. It uses the word *homily* in a broad sense.
According to the *Ordo*, "the homily explains the biblical Word of God proclaimed
in the readings or some other text of the liturgy."

and actualization of the Word of God for the benefit of the celebrating community.

In the liturgy of the synagogue, the connection between the Word of God and the homily is so intimate that the orator normally begins his homily with the formula: "This is what Scripture says," or "This is what is written."[2] They are superb formulas, for they impose on the speaker the welcome obligation of returning unceasingly to Scripture, to prolonging the Word of God by his human word.

One may also note that only Judaism and the two religions that have developed from it, Christianity and Islam, use the homily as an essential element in their celebration. Judaism, which underwent the destruction of the Temple in A.D. 70, so that the ministry of priests in the Temple ceased, has survived all its agonies thanks to the homilies of the rabbis who explained the Word to the people in every synagogal office. Islam did not know a priesthood properly speaking; it drew its vitality—sometimes its aggressiveness—from the words of the imans who explained the Koran to the people. Christianity knew both the presbyteral ministry (in the service of the Eucharist) and the ministry of the Word. In countries long Christianized, these two ministries are normally exercised by the same person. It is vain to ask which ministry is the most important: the service of the Eucharist or the service of the Word. The two are necessary. But one may say that of two communities, one of which would have Mass without a homily, and the other a homily without Mass, and this for a length of time, the most Christian community would be that which had kept the homily.[3]

While underlining here the importance of the homily, we must not underestimate other ways of celebrating the Word. Their efficacy may be even greater than that of the homily.

We are thinking especially of the Lutheran cantata. At the summit of thes cantatas are the Passions of J. S. Bach: that according to St. John (performed for the first time on April 7, 1724) and that according to St. Matthew, "the most exalting and the most important monument to evangelical music"[4] (performed for the first time on March 30, 1736). Into the woof of the Gospel text given by the

[2] Strack-Billerbeck, *Kommentar zum Neuen Testament, aus Talmud und Midrasch,* C. H. Beck, München, vol. IV, 1961, 173.

[3] J. W. Cox, *The Impact of Worship on Preaching* in *Preaching and Worship,* Princeton Theological Seminary, Princeton, N.J. 1980, 17.

[4] Selon A. Basso, *Jean-Sébastien Bach,* Fayard, vol. II, 1985, 525.

evangelista, Bach has inserted not only ancient Lutheran chorals which keep the devotion of the assembly on its toes, but also solo airs *(soliloquentes)* in which he expresses an ardent piety, and the interventions of the crowd *(turba)* which intensify the sacred drama to a high degree and transform the account into an intense celebration of the Passion. The unforgettable *Messiah* of G. F. Handel (performed for the first time in Dublin on April 13, 1742) presents a history of salvation. Performed unceasingly ever since, never worn out, always fresh, it has proclaimed for two and a half centuries, the richest pages of the Bible. Closer to us in time is the admirable meditation on death of J. Brahms in the *German Requiem* (1868): the work radiates the peace of heaven. It is uniquely constructed from the best biblical texts. It reveals the wretchedness of certain verses of the *Dies Irae,* "day of anger" according to the testimony of the Sybil *(teste David cum Sybilla!).* From the first day of their creation, these masterworks—veritable musical homilies—have inscribed the Word of God in the hearts of innumerable faithful. They have often redeemed by their irresistible beauty the insipidity and mediocrity of "official" homilies.

Formerly, use of the Latin language did not permit Catholic assemblies to follow the practice of the Protestant Churches. But since Vatican II opened the entrance of the sanctuary to living languages, there has been a veritable explosion of biblical canticles: some are authentic proclamations of the Word of God. Thanks to the magic of music, the Word is forever inscribed in the memory of the faithful. Unknown before the Council, the text "Remember Jesus Christ, the Risen One" is known and proclaimed today throughout the world.[5]

Let us also mention sculpture and stained glass. Those of the Middle Ages move us and enchant us still today, and transform our ancient cathedrals into illustrated Bibles. Those of the cathedral at Chartres, for example, have a richness which is unique. When the midday sun embraces the south face with its fire and makes the blue of the stained glass sing, it seems as if the people portrayed in the glass come to life.

At a time where audiovisual means have taken on such importance, we must not neglect any possibility. We must invent new

---

[5] After 2 Tim 2:8-12, note that the Catholic liturgy, totally centered on the celebration of the Mass, offers no space for welcoming for the biblical works such as *King David* by A. Honegger (words by R. Morex).

ones so that "the Word of the Lord may accomplish its course and be glorified."[6]

The radiation and diffusion of the Word in the celebration

Besides the homily properly speaking, there exist other possibilities of radiating and diffusing the Word during the celebration. There is the greeting and the blessing at the beginning of Mass, which may base itself on the Word, the penitential preparation which may draw its inspiration from the Word, the introductions to the readings, which, if they are "simple, faithful to the text, brief, and prepared with care,"[7] furnish precious keys to understanding, the prayer of the faithful, which may draw its intercessions from the readings, the introduction to the Our Father, the invitation to communion, the prayer of thanksgiving, the closing formula.[8] The Word must not be imprisoned in the readings and in the homily. If it is truly the foundation on which the Covenant is built, if the Eucharist is the celebration of the new Covenant, it is normal that it should be present throughout the celebration.

THE HOMILY OF JESUS AND THE HOMILY OF EZRA

The homily of Ezra

These interventions must not be "mini-homilies" that tire the assembly, but rather they should give it rest by making an echo of the Word of God resound in its heart.

In its simplest form the homily is the translation of the Word of God for the benefit of the celebrating community. The most significant example of this kind of homily is the solemn reading of the Law by Ezra in 445 to the exiles who had just returned from captivity in Babylon.[9] This gathering has been called "the day of

[6] 2 Thess 3:1.
[7] *OLM*, 15.
[8] See the formulas that we have proposed in *Reflections of His Word, Cycles A, B, C*, Schiller Park, Ill., World Library, 1980.
[9] On the assembly of Nehemiah, see L. Deiss, *God's Word and God's People*, Collegeville, The Liturgical Press, 1976. We take up here certain elements of this work concerning the Jewish homily and the Christian homily. On the New Testament, see P. Grelot et M. Dumais, *Homélies sur l'Écriture à l'époque apostolique*, Desclée, 1989.

the birth of Judaism." It is related in one of the most beautiful pages
in the Book of Nehemiah:

> The people gathered in the square before the Water Gate. They
> told the scribe Ezra to bring the book of the Law of Moses that the
> Lord had given to Israel. The priest Ezra brought the Law before
> the assembly, both men and women and all who could hear with
> understanding. It was on the first day of the seventh month.
> He read from it from early morning until noon, in the presence
> of the men and women and those who could understand. The ears
> of all the people were attentive to the book of the Law. . . .
> Then Ezra blessed the Lord, the great God, and all the people
> answered, "Amen, Amen," lifting up their hands. Then they bowed
> and prostrated themselves before Yahweh, their faces to the ground.
> (Joshua, Bani, Sherebiah, Jamin, Akkub, Shabbethai, Hodiah,
> Maaseiah, Kelita, Azariah, Jozabad, Hanan, Pelaiah, the levites,
> helped the people to understand the Law, while the people remained
> in their places).
> So Ezra read from the book, from the Law of God, interpreting
> it and giving the sense: thus the people understood the reading.
> (Neh 8:1-8)

In 587–586 the armies of Nebuchadnezzar smashed down the
walls of Jerusalem, set the city on fire, made blood run, and deported a main part of the population to Babylon. In 538, Cyrus
signed an edict which allowed the exiles, in successive caravans,
to return to the Holy Land. In 445 (?), Nehemiah, born during the
deportation and having become the delegate of Artaxerxes I (465–
424), king of Persia, obtained authorization to go to Jerusalem to
consolidate the religious restoration among the repatriated people.
The solemn reading of the Law represented a capital moment in
this restoration.

Nehemiah proclaimed the sacred text in Hebrew. This tongue,
especially since the deportation, had become somewhat archaic. The
returning people—descendants of those who had been deported in
587–586, a century and a half beforehand—had had to adopt the
language of their masters, Aramaic, the dominant language of
Assyrio-Babylonia.[10] It was therefore necessary to translate the He-

---

[10] According to M. Carrez, Aramaic was, in about 500, "the official language of
the chancelleries of the Persian empire (*Les langues de la Bible*, Centurion, Paris, 1983,
31).

brew text into several dialects of Aramaic for the deportation had "mixed" Israel with the nations. It had also mixed the languages. Nehemiah recounts: "I saw Jews who had married Ashdodite, Ammonite and Moabite women." As for their children, half spoke Ashdodian or the tongue of this or that people, but no longer knew how to speak Judean.[11]

The tradition liked to trace back to Nehemiah the origin of the *Targum*, a Hebrew word which means "translation." The Aramaic translation of the Hebrew was used in the synagogal liturgy.[12] First the sacred text was read in Hebrew, then its translation was given in Aramaic. On the historical level, the affirmation according to which the *Targum* originated in the assembly of Nehemiah is unverifiable. But with or without the assembly of Nehemiah, the translation of the Hebrew into a living language was an absolute necessity: the descendants of the exiles of 587–586, who returned to Palestine after the edict of Cyrus in 538 until the assembly of Nehemiah in 445, had been speaking Aramaic for more than a century, thus for several generations.

For the understanding of the biblical texts, the *Targum* is extremely important. In fact, no translation is innocent, none approaches the Hebrew text in a virginal manner. The translation reads the text through the prism of the translator. The *Targum* is not therefore a doublet of the Hebrew Bible. It already presents a certain interpretation, or an interpretive translation.[13] "The one who translates absolutely literally is a falsifier; the one who adds something is a blasphemer.[14] It is sometimes difficult to measure the distance which separates the translation from the interpretation, the falsifier from the blasphemer. In fact, we possess in the *Targums* the interpretation of the Bible according to the tradition of Israel, most often according to the heart of its best adherents. Here we have the beginning of the homily.

The chronicler who edited the Books of Ezra and Nehemiah, worked in the third century, thus a century and a half after the events. Without doubt he introduced into his account the usages

---

[11] Neh 13:23-24 (Ashdodian is probably a dialect of Aramaic).

[12] See R. Le Déaut, *Introduction à la littérature targumique*, Institut Biblique Pontifical, Rome, 1966. The author analyzes Neh 8:8, and the linguistic situation in Palestin after the Exile, 23–32.

[13] P. Grelot, dans *Cahiers Évangile*, supplement to 54, 5.

[14] Cited by R. Le Déaut, in *Introduction à la littérature targumique, op. cit.*, 43.

of the synagogal liturgy of his time.[15] In fact, the assembly of Nehemiah did not resemble in any way a community that was content with listening peaceably to the Word: the community stood up, it lifted its hands, it ratified the blessings pronounced by Nehemiah by its *Amens*, it prostrated itself, faces to the ground. It was a question then, not of a simple reading of the Law, but of an authentic celebration of the Word.

Two lists of names bring no understanding to the text, but they are very significant. Those who surrounded Nehemiah as assessors, remind us that the readings of the synagogal service were not read by a single reader, but by three during ordinary services, and by seven on feast days and sabbaths. This signifies that individuals were not bearers of the Word but the community itself. It was the people as a whole who proclaimed the Word, and the people as a whole who heard it. God spoke through the community.

The same significance must be given to the presence of the levites who explain the Law. The verse is considered as an overload. In confiding the task of explaining the Law to "his dear levites"[16] the chronicler underlined their importance for the cult. He affirmed at the same time that it was truly the community which explained the Law to the community.

The homily of Jesus at Nazareth

In its most simple form, the homily is the translation of the Word. In its most perfect form, the homily is the actualization of the Word for the celebrating community. The archetypal example here is Jesus' homily in the synagogue at Nazareth. Luke recounts:[17]

> He went to Nazareth, where he had been brought up, and on the sabbath day he went into the synagogue, as was his custom. And he stood up to read. The scroll of the prophet Isaiah was handed to him. Unrolling it, he found the place where it is written:
> "The Spirit of the Lord is upon me, because he has anointed me to preach good news to the poor. He has sent me to proclaim free-

---

[15] F. Michaeli, *Les livres des Chroniques, d'Esdras et de Néhémie*, coll. "Commentaire de l'Ancien Testament," XVI, Éd. Delachaux et Niestlé, 1967, 336–337.

[16] The word is that of A. Lefèvre, "Néhémie et Esdras," in D.B.S., vol. VI, 1960, col. 408.

[17] The text of Luke 4:16-30 seems to regroup three visits that Jesus made to Nazareth. The first is that which we cite here, Luke 4:16-22a. The second, Luke 4:22b-24, is found

dom for captives and recovery of sight for the blind; to release the oppressed; to proclaim a year of the Lord's favor."
Then he rolled up the scroll, gave it back to the attendant and sat down. The eyes of everyone in the synagogue were fastened on him, and he said to them, "Today this scripture is fulfilled in your hearing." And everyone gave witness to him. They marvelled at the gracious words that came from his mouth.

(4:16-22)

The heart of the synagogal celebration was the reading of a pericope (*seder*) of the Law or Torah, that is, from the Pentateuch. This reading was followed by a reading from the prophets or *haftarah*, which was chosen to be a commentary on the Law. Luke was familiar with the structure of these celebrations. During the mission of Paul to Antioch of Pisidia, he writes:

On the sabbath day, they (Paul and Barnabas) entered the synagogue and sat down. After the reading of the Law and the Prophets the elders of the synagogue sent word to them: "Brothers, if you have some word of consolation for the people, speak." Thus Paul stood up, motioned with his hand and said . . . (Acts 13:15-16)

In the account of the visit to Nazareth, Luke has organized his text with great literary perfection. Everything develops like a well organized liturgical office:

A   He stood up
B   They gave him
C   Having opened the book
            The Spirit of the Lord is upon *me*
            Because he has anointed *me*
            He has sent *me*
C'   Having rolled up the scroll
B'   Having given it back to the attendant
A'   He sat down.

By using the chiasm (AB . . . B' A'), which placed Jesus in the center of the account, Luke underlines his messianic activity: the Spirit rests upon him, he receives anointing, he is sent to announce the Good News to the poor.

in the parallels of Matt 13:54-58 and Mark 6:1-6. The third, Luke 4:25-30, appears to belong to Luke's own sources. The first visit evokes wonder, (Luke 4:22) the second, scandal (Mark 6:3) the third, an attempt at assassination, (Luke 4:29).

Jesus reads the second reading (*haftarah*), from the prophets. But the text as Luke gives it is not to be found in the Book of the Prophets. Luke combines Isaiah 61:1 and 61:2. He omits "to cure broken hearts," which is found in Isaiah 61:1. He adds "to announce deliverance to the oppressed," which is found in Isaiah 58:6. He has reworked the source he uses.[18] With what mastery!

> The Spirit of the *Lord* is upon me
> *To proclaim* to captives
>   *deliverance,*
>   sight to the blind
>   *deliverance* to the oppressed
> *To proclaim* a year of grace
> of the *Lord.*

Clearly the readers of Luke's Gospel are more blessed than those who listened to Jesus! The messianic activity is described with a literary elegance of which the Nazareans could never have suspected![19]

Jesus stands up to read the reading from the Prophets. The *hazzan* (attendant) hands him back the scroll of Isaiah. Had the text been prepared by the *hazzan*? If so, Jesus had only to open the scroll. If not, Jesus would have had to find his text. Ch. Perrot notes: "One does not open a scroll as one opens a book, at no matter what page! Jesus would have had to gently unroll more than five meters of the scroll, at least, before *finding* his text. A scroll begins at the end, and as here it is a question of Isaiah 61:1 ff . . . . In fact, the text *found* by Jesus was a *chosen* text."[20]

When Jesus finished reading the text from the Prophets (Luke quotes only the beginning) while the eyes of all the assembly are fixed on him, he declares: "Today this Scripture is accomplished in your hearing." Let us understand: "Today this Word which you have just heard is accomplished." This today of Jesus in the synagogue at Nazareth is at the heart of every homily. Every word spoken before the community is the word that God speaks today to the community.

---

[18] The vocabulary used is linked with that of Acts. See P. Benoit, M.-E. Boismard, *Synopse des Quatre Évangiles,* vol. II, Éd. du Cerf, Paris, 1972, 90.

[19] See J.-N. Aletti, "Jésus à Nazareth," in *A cause de l'Évangile,* coll. "Lectio Divina," 123, 1985, 431–451.

[20] C. Perrot, *op. cit.,* 139–140.

The homily of Nehemiah at Jerusalem dates from about the year 445. The homily of Jesus at Nazareth from the year 28, at the beginning of his public ministry. In spite of the 473 years—almost five centuries—which separate the two homilies, the aim of the homily is always to translate the Word of God by making clear its actuality.

FROM TRANSLATION TO ACTUALIZATION

The path which leads from Nehemiah's homily at Jerusalem to that of Jesus at Nazareth, that is to say, from a simple translation of the Word to its actualization, involves "obligatory passages."

Literal sense

The first step is to look at the literal meaning. Any other starting point is arbitrary and leads everywhere and nowhere. The first question is always: What do we find written here? What is being said by the text? Vatican II observes: "The interpreter of sacred Scripture must carefully search out the meaning which the sacred writers really wanted to communicate and that God was pleased to communicate through the medium of their words."[21]

This is the task of the exegete. He must be humble enough to apply textual criticism (are there variants?); literary criticism (what is the literary genre of the account?); historical criticism (how situate the event in the context of history?), and theological criticism (how does the text fit into revelation?). Lack of such criteria makes one dream in the wastelands of fantastic interpretations. One risks, for example, confounding a parable with history, or, scarcely better, history with a parable. Who can say what harm has been done by an "historical" interpretation of the serpent in Genesis or the whale of Jonah? Who could dispute that these images, which still haunt the unconscious of certain members of the faithful, have thrown discredit on other more essential revelations of the Bible? To define the literal meaning is always an urgent necessity. The interpretation of the Bible is a rigorous science, not a game for pious

---

[21] Constitution on Divine Revelation, *Dei Verbum*, 12.

dabblers. It is an operational science "in the sense that each reader can practice for himself the operations that led the exegetes to their conclusions."[22]

In exegesis, then, there can be no skimping of serious study of the Bible; that study is also a form of praise and prayer. There are still communities and preachers who suffer from underdevelopment as far as the Bible is concerned. We are not saying, of course, that every page of the Bible is full of traps and requires exhaustive study. The Bible remains the book of the poor and simple, even though at the same time it lends itself to technical study. Nor is it a question in the homily of presenting the community with the immediate results of scholarly work, parading one's knowledge before the assembly. All we are saying is that intellectual honesty requires that one have some idea of what one is talking about, and therefore that each Christian ought to study the Bible according to their capacities of time, situation, and intelligence.

The new Lectionary has revealed to our communities almost all of the most difficult biblical problems. They must be treated with humility and prudence so as not to wound the faith of the little ones, precisely those to whom the Father reveals his mystery.[23] Origen was already conscious of this problem: "I pass on to you something a wise man and true believer said to me; I think of it often. He said: 'It is dangerous to talk about God, even if what you say is true. It is not only false ideas that are dangerous; even true ones are if they are not expressed at the right time.'"[24]

Yet prudence works in both directions. It is dangerous to speak too soon, but it may be even more dangerous to keep silent and avoid difficult questions by smothering them in commonplaces, or, even worse, sugarcoating them with pious platitudes. There are attitudes which cloak themselves in the mantle of prudence, but which are really acts of cowardice. The faithful ask questions about the historical character of the Infancy Narratives and about what really happened at the baptism or temptation or transfiguration of Jesus (to mention only some New Testament problems). They do not accept the idea of a biblical paradise in which the "elect" have free access to the springs of living water, while the ordinary believer

---

[22] H. Cazelles, *Écriture, Parole et Esprit*, Desclée, 1970, 108.

[23] Matt 11:25.

[24] *Homélies sur Ézékiel*, I, 11. —Cf. *SC*, 352, 1989, p. 80. On Origen as preacher, see P. Nautin in *SC*, 232, 1976, 100–191.

must be content with the stagnant water of old cisterns. Such questions are healthy. They should receive clear answers, given with an exemplary fidelity to honest exegesis. There is no shame in saying, when confronted with this or that difficulty, "I don't know the answer," or "No generally accepted solution has yet been found." What is intolerable is the lie calculated to make others believe one knows when one does not.

To summarize: the first veneration towards the Bible, the first praise given to the Word of God, is the search for its literal meaning. God speaks to me; I adore him by welcoming his Word in its literal meaning. In this search the duty of an exegetical master is no different from that of a catechist in the African bush who has no biblical formation: each one must seek out the literal meaning according to their charism, according to intellectual capacity, availability of helpful biblical aids, and of time. In a word, one must seek the meaning according to his or her possibilities. For the literal sense retains its richness, whatever the level of approach. All this is simply a question of common sense.

Christological sense

The second step is that of the Christological meaning. Christ fulfills the Scriptures; his presence illumines every page of the Bible. The homily's task is to reveal this presence to the community.

It is here that the Christian homily separates itself from the Jewish homily. Throughout its history the Jewish tradition discovered with awe the riches of the Word. But it stopped just before the time of the New Testament. It stumbled against the tomb of Christ. Anxiously it questioned God:

Will you work your wonders for the dead?
Will the shades stand and praise you? (Ps 88:11).

God responded to this question by the resurrection of Jesus. Christian faith, born on Easter morning, continues to marvel at the Word even more than the Jewish tradition, for it reads every page in the light of the resurrection of Christ.

The account of the pilgrims of Emmaus magnificently insists on the presence of the risen Christ at the heart of the Scriptures. Jesus reproaches the disciples who journey with him:

O spirits without understanding and hearts slow to believe
all the prophets foretold! (Luke 24:25).

And Luke continues:

And having begun with Moses
and with all the prophets,
he interpreted in all the Scriptures
the things concerning him (Luke 24:27).

Notice the insistence on the totality of Scripture: "*All* that the
prophets foretold . . . . *All* the prophets . . . *all* the Scriptures."
One asks how Jesus could have gone through *all* the Scriptures, explained *all* the prophets on the way to Jerusalem. Clearly, this is
a theological affirmation: *all the Scriptures* announce and reveal
the mystery of Jesus. Faith in the risen Jesus gives understanding
of *all* the Scriptures.

We find the same insistence on the totality of Scripture in the
last instructions that Jesus addresses to his disciples just before the
Ascension.

All that has been written of me
in the Law of Moses, the Prophets
and the Psalms must be accomplished (Luke 24:44).

Jesus cites the Scriptures according to the classification generally used at his time. One distinguished the Law or *Torah*, the
Prophets or *Nebiim*, and the Writings or *Ketûbîm*.

By the Law or *Torah* one understood the Pentateuch. These first
five books were attributed to the authorship of Moses. Thus, we
have the term "Law of Moses." They were considered as the heart
of the Word of God.

Among the Prophets or *Nebiim*, one distinguished the first or
former prophets (which are the books which we count among the
historical books: Joshua, Judges, Samuel and Kings: history is thus
considered as a prophecy of the Messiah), and the latter prophets
(Isaiah, Jeremiah, Ezekiel and Daniel, and the twelve "minor"
prophets).

The writings or *Ketûbîm* made up the rest of the Bible. The Book
of Psalms is the most important among the collection. Jesus uses
metonymy when he speaks of Psalms to designate the whole collection of the Writings.

There is therefore, according the faith of the primitive community, a history of Jesus in the Pentateuch, a history of Jesus in the Prophets, and a history of Jesus in the Psalms. And we are invited in the footsteps of the apostles to discover on each page of the Law, the Prophets, and the Psalms, the face of Jesus. Irenaeus summed it up: "The writings of Moses are the words of Christ."[25]

We must notice, however, that an exact citation of the prophecies that Jesus is said to have accomplished according to the primitive tradition, is deceiving;[26] it gives only a pale trace of the richness of his person. How can we affirm that he has accomplished all the Scriptures when certain books of the Old Testament are not even cited in the New? We are reminded of what Pascal said: "In these promises, each finds what is in the depths of their heart."[27] It is, in fact, the incarnation and especially the resurrection which accomplishes *all the Scriptures*. Jesus himself, the Risen One, gives his own the key to understanding the Scriptures: "He opened their minds to the understanding of the Scriptures."[28] The ancient text of Scripture remains. But the resurrection of Jesus transfigures it and gives it a new meaning.

Certainly, Jewish hope too lived in expectation of the resurrection. Jesus himself shared the richness of this hope: "The God of Abraham, Isaac, and Jacob is not a God of the dead but of the living."[29] But the resurrection, a gift of the Father, is infinitely more than a return to life, even an eternal life. It establishes Jesus, "born of the seed of David, Son of God with might, according to the spirit of holiness."[30] It shows forth in "Jesus, a man himself,"[31] "the beloved Son of the Father."

Without the resurrection of Jesus, the history of Israel remains weeping at the Wailing Wall in Jerusalem, and Christians would never have left the Jewish synagogues. With the resurrection, the history of Israel springs forth again in that of the Church, and the

---

[25] *Against the Heresies*, IV:2, 3. Cf. SC, 100, 1965, 400.
[26] See B. Lauret, "Christologie dogmatique" in *Initiation à la pratique de la théologie*, vol. 2, Cerf, Paris, 1982, 301–302.
[27] Paschal, *Pensées*.
[28] J. Ernst in *Evangelium nach Lukas* (Pustet, 1977) writes: "For Luke, the decisive principle for the interpretation of Scripture is faith in the Resurrection of Jesus; it is the basis for the proclamation to the community."
[29] Luke 20:37-38.
[30] Rom 1:3-4.
[31] 1 Tim 2:5.

Risen One, transfigured by the glory of heaven, leads all his sisters and brothers to his Father.

Without this resurrection, Abraham would still sleep in peace next to his beautiful Sarah, in the dust of the tomb of Makpelah, with Isaac and Rebecca, Leah and Jacob. With this resurrection, he enters, glorified, with all those he loves, into the heaven of Jesus Christ.

Without this resurrection, the heroes of suffering, a cortege of sombre beauty whose tears wet every page of the Psalter, would have had only the silence which surrounded the Cross of Jesus as a reply to their suffering. With this resurrection, their tears appear as seeds of an eternity of glory.

Without this resurrection, the phrases of the Gospel and their sense of eternity would appear as only the dream of a visionary dreamer. For who would dare to affirm that the poor are blessed if there would not be a future resurrection? But today the poor know that they will receive the Kingdom on the day of resurrection.

Without the resurrection of Jesus, we should celebrate no liturgy, and the recommendation: "Do this in memory of me" would remain a dead letter, for one does not remember someone who is dead on a cross. But today, the glorified Christ is alive and living in the midst of every community.

Without the resurrection, the world and its stardust would turn unceasingly in the emptiness of the cosmos, without ever progressing. With the resurrection of Jesus, the world is being brought to birth, preparing its rebirth as a new heaven and a new earth.

The resurrection of Jesus is at the center of Scripture It is also at the heart of the universe, at the center of billions of light-years; it is the ultimate explanation of the world. It is the Word which existed before everything "in the beginning" and in which all things draw their existence."[32] Jesus gives meaning to the universe, to Scripture, and to our own existence.

Actualization

The last step or stage is that of actualization. It is also the richest stage, and that which may be the most diversified. One may obtain a certain exegetical consensus concerning the literal sense (a

[32] John 1:1-2.

single meaning is given) and the Christological sense (a single accomplishment is realized in Christ). But once actualization begins, the text may open up a thousand diverse paths.

Actualization is the heart of the homily. Every community must hear the Word in its own way. It must take the word of Jesus and adapt it thus: "Today this word, to which we have just listened, is accomplished for us." Ways of actualizing the readings are multiple, unlimited in their possibilities, as are the situations of the readers which they address.[33]

Each age must hear the Word in its own way. Each generation must experience the mystery of the contemporaneity of the Word for all times. The total meaning of the Word will only be fully revealed when God closes the book of history at the end of time and reveals himself no longer through the Word, but in an eternal face to face. Then the contemporaneity of the Word will give way to the eternity of God.

Actualization forces us to raise once again the difficult problem of translation. What does it mean to translate a text? Sometimes people have thought it simply means passing from Hebrew, Aramaic, and Greek, to the living languages. Of course, such a passage is necessary. The translation experts are always trying to improve their work, so that their text is as faithful as possible to the original, inspired by the Spirit of God. Yet the translation of which we speak in connection with the homily, makes other kinds of demand. It aims to insert God's message into the life of the community, to make it penetrate the sensibility, understanding, concerns, joys, and troubles of the community. To translate God's Word is, as it were, to incarnate it in a particular community.

Sometimes a certain priest or believer will say that this or that passage of the Bible is not suitable for their community. In making such a statement, these unfortunate people are simply admitting that they have not given a successful homily, since their task, after all, is precisely the daunting but joyful ministry of translating the Word for the benefit of the community. Christ needs their words if he is to address their community, just as he needs the priest's hands in order to break the Eucharistic bread and share it among the faithful. In the homily, the whole community is gathered before the

[33] M. Dumais, L'actualisation du Nouveau Testament, coll. "Lectio Divina," 107, 1981, 91–92.

Word, looks at itself as if in a mirror, and discovers in the mirror the face of Jesus.

The homily, consequently, cannot be reduced to a matter of simply giving historical explanations of the text; these may be quite useful in situating the event in its biblical context, but they do not constitute a homily. Nor does a homily consist in explaining Palestinian geography, though some details of such information may be quite relevant. Nor does it consist in explaining biblical vocabulary, or scriptural themes, or moral exhortations, however useful they may be. All these are only crutches to help us enter into the presence of Christ. The homily begins exactly when the community encounters Christ.

The homily is not even meant to be explanation, however excellent. Just as God does not want to play the historian for us, even though he is the master of history, or the geographer, even though he creates the universe, or the philologist, even though he invented human language, neither does he intend to act as our theologian, even though he is God! Consequently, explaining to the community that there are three Persons in God (a point of theology), or, in more detail, that God is a Father, that he has sent his Son among us, and that the Spirit has descended into our world (these three statements are the scriptural way of expressing the mystery of the Trinity) is not what constitues a homily. For a real homily begins only at the point when we understand that this Word has been fulfilled *today for us*, and that God, the Father of our Lord Jesus Christ is today our Father, that his Son Jesus Christ has become today our brother, and that the Spirit has been sent to live today in our hearts. The tripartite structure—literal meaning, Christological meaning, and actualization—is fundamental. However, according to the needs and situation of the community, and according to the biblical text given, emphasis may be placed on the literal sense or the Christological sense or the actualization of the text. The homily is never a ready-made affair, but must be tailored to serve the needs of the community.

THE HOMILY OF EACH CELEBRATION

The principle that every time the Word is proclaimed that it must be actualized holds true. In practice this means that there should be a homily at every Mass and at every celebration of the Word. The community present need not be large. We should recall that according to the Gospel, two or three people form a fine community: "Where two or three are gathered in my name, there am I in their midst."[34] Without this actualization, the Bible remains a library in which Israel and the apostles are the librarians. Now, a library is only a source of knowledge if the books speak. If not, it is a cemetery. Hence it is essential that through the homily the Bible becomes Word.

The homily need not be long. Two or three minutes can be enough. In fact, as a general rule, if the homily is well prepared, it can be short. The homilist must take time to prepare it and be brief in giving it.

Evidently, no one can preach a daily sermon. The homilist would quickly exhaust his knowledge and would literally have nothing more to say. But a daily homily, a real homily, is the simplest thing in the world. No one need fear that they will be worn out by the effort. No one grows tired gazing daily upon the face of Jesus Christ.

The real problem is not with having a daily homily, but with its quality.

ALL THE TEXTS?

We have already posed the question of the number of readings: three readings on Sundays and feasts, two readings on weekdays, plus the psalm. Must the homily explain and actualize all the texts?

The same question can be asked even in regard to a single reading. The message is sometimes so rich or so dense that there is enough to provide material for several homilies. Must we be exhaustive and speak of everything?

The table of the Word is a royal table, marvellously laden, to which God invites the beggars whom he loves. To do honor to the host, each guest need not fill his plate at every course and suffer indigestion. Therefore, eat what you please and as much as you please. God wants the homilist to experience joy, not fatigue. It is therefore not necessary to speak of all the texts; it is enough to

---

[34] Matt 18:20.

speak for the sake of the community and to feed it, according to its hunger.

THE HOMILY, WORD OF GOD

The homily is not simply a human discourse about God, but is itself a word of God. It does not, of course, have the universal value of the Word in which the Church, according to the canon of the Scriptures, recognizes God's authentic voice addressing all humankind. A homily to one community may not necessarily be deliverable to all other communities. Nonetheless, the homily remains the word of God to the celebrating community. The homily should be simply an amplification of the concrete time in which we live, the most wonderful time of all, since it is the "today" of God for us, of God's eternal Word. "If someone speaks, let them deliver God's message."[35] And the one who hears should receive what is said as God's Word. "You have welcomed the Word," Paul says to the Thessalonians, "not as a human word, but as it truly is: the Word of God."[36]

The *Targum* tradition gives numerous examples of homiletic texts become word of God.[37] In principle, the translator (*meturgeman*) had to translate the Hebrew text literally into Aramaic. In practice, they interpreted the original text, enriching it, sometimes profiting from the opportunity offered to insert some personal ideas of their own. Certain of these new additions, pious inventions of the human mind, are sometimes taken up in the New Testament, accorded the dignity of texts inspired by the Holy Spirit, and become part of the Gospel. Luke gives a superb example when he cites the Word of Jesus in his inaugural sermon:

> *Be merciful*
> *as your heavenly Father is merciful* (Luke 6:36).

This law shines like the light of the evangelical Law. It represents the summit of Christian action. It is the sublime rule by which the merciful person imitates the infinite mercy of the Father! Jesus alone

[35] 1 Pet 4:11.
[36] 1 Thess 2:13.
[37] See L. Deiss, *God's Word and God's People.*

could invent it. He alone, the Merciful one, could proclaim it, we think. But in fact, it is not Jesus who invented this evangelical law, but a targumist. One day, in a poor and unknown Judean or Galilean synagogue, perhaps even in Babylon, during an unpretentious service that has left no trace in history, an unknown targumist, whose name is forever lost to Israel's memory, had to translate a banal legislative text of Leviticus, a text concerning the fate of cows and their young: "Cow or sheep, you shall not slay with its calf, on the same day" (Lev 22:28). An insignificant text for Yahwistic faith, making allusion to a Canaanite custom.[38] The translator added to the Aramaic translation this thought, springing forth from the very heart of God:

> My people, children of Israel!
> as I am merciful in heaven,
> so you shall be merciful on earth.[39]

And thus, this word of a humble targumist with a heart of gold and a soul fired by the Spirit of God, was taken up by Jesus in his inaugural sermon and became a word of the Gospel. Human word become Word of God. Homily become Gospel.

If only each of the words of our homilies might appear likewise as a word of Jesus! If only the entire community which celebrates the Word might become an epiphany of the Gospel, revelation of the mercy of God towards the world!

LITERARY GENRES AND FORMS

In the Bible, Israel utilized the most diverse literary genres, even those which were in use in the neighboring literatures and of which the hidden hieroglyphics of the sands of Egypt or the cuniform tablets of the Mesopotamian ruins have revealed marvellous examples.

The oldest literary genre is undoubtedly the myth. The best biblical examples of it are the creation accounts in the opening chapters of Genesis. The historical genre is subdivided into documentary history, based on the royal archives or the temple archives as in 1 Kings; epic history, as in the patriarchal narratives; and thematic

---

[38] M. Noth, *Das dritte Buch Mose*, Vandenhoeck & Ruprecht, Göttingen, 1966, 142.
[39] *Targum du Pentateuque*, SC, 256, 1979, 475. Trad. R. Le Déaut.

history, as in the work of the chronicler. The lyric genre is found especially in the Psalms, the didactic genre in the Wisdom literature, the juridical genre in Leviticus, the apocalyptic genre in the Book of Daniel, and the epistolary genre in the Letters of Paul. These literary genres are seldom found in their pure state. Often, they have been mixed one with another and have mutually enriched each other. Within the same genre, what diversities! There is a whole world between the prayer of Psalm 88, where the person praying controls his agony, and the confessions where Jeremiah wails his despair, although both texts are lamentations. A world too between the Letter to Philemon, where Paul intercedes—and with what tenderness!—for a run-away slave, and the Letter to the Romans which is a theological treatise.

The homily is a human echo of God's Word. It may therefore adopt all the literary genres of the text it actualizes. It may be intense poetry, like the admirable homily of Melito of Sardis on the Pasch,[40] or simple catechetical instruction, like the homilies of Origen, which are just as admirable. What is required is simply that it is concerned, through the architecture of language, with the fundamental affirmation: this is what God is saying today to the community.

Beauty, composed of simplicity and truth is fitting for the homily. If only we could present God's Word as on a golden platter! Literary beauty is also a creature of God[41] and should be drafted into the service of the Word, like all other forms of beauty. Think of the fierce beauty of Amos, the limpid splendor of Isaiah, the passionate tenderness of Jeremiah, the sweetness of the Song of Songs. Above all, think of Jesus and the seduction his words exercized. One said of him: "Never has a man spoken like this man!"[42] In our own day, his parables still seem marvellously fresh and natural, as if they were being uttered for the first time. Of course, too great a literary richness would be just as blameworthy as neglect of literary form. True beauty is the sister of simplicity.

[40] This homily dates from the years 160–170 according to O. Perler, *Méliton de Sardes, Sur la Pâque*, SC 123, 1966.
[41] Augustine notes that the joy of those who speak makes what they say more relaxed and more persuasive *facilius atque acceptius. De catechizandis rudibus*, II, 4, coll. "Oeuvres de saint Augustin," J. Longère, *La prédication médiévale*, Études augustiniennes, Paris, 1983, 33–34.
[42] John 7:46.

THE MINISTER OF THE HOMILY

Who may or who must give the homily? This question has two sides. One is legislative. According to canon law, "the ministry of the Word of God" is entrusted to all the baptized.[43] But the homily itself, "eminent form of preaching" in which the mysteries of faith are explained from their base in the sacred texts (*ex textu sacro fidei mysteria*), is reserved to priests and deacons.[44] It is normal that the bishop, "whose first charge, among his principal duties, is the preaching of the gospel,"[45] should watch over homilies given in liturgical celebrations for which he bears responsibility. In his diocese he is "moderator of all ministry of the Word."[46]

The other side of the question freely asks: what is the ideal for the community? May we dream that the time will come when, after the reading of the Word, the presider will address the assembly in the words once used in the synagogue of Antioch in Pisidia: "Sisters and brothers, if you have some word of consolation to address to the people, please speak up."[47] Will we ever carry out in the liturgy—not only with the approbation of the bishop, but with his encouragement and blessing—the recommendation of the primitive tradition: "In wisdom made perfect, instruct and admonish one another."[48]

It is fitting to remember that it is the whole Church—and not merely the ordained priesthood or the hierarchy—which celebrates the Word and shares in the priestly, prophetic, and kingly function of Christ. Vatican II explains:

> Christ, great prophet . . . accomplishes this prophetic function not only through the hierarchy which teaches in his name and with his

[43] Code of Canon Law, 1983, 756–759.
[44] Code of Canon Law, 767, 1.
[45] *Lumen Gentium*, 25.
[46] Code 756. The *Directory for Sunday Assemblies in the Absence of a Priest*, 43, (2 June, 1988) recalls this norm. The French translation (Cerf. 1988, 40) adds a note saying that the Conference of the French bishops "has established that a layperson may be admitted to preach: they must have the desired preparation and be designated by the Ordinary, for a maximum period of three years, renewable." For the decisions of the German episcopal conference 24 February 1988, see *DC*, 85, 1988, 840–841.
[47] Acts 13:15.
[48] Col 3:16.

authority, but also through laypeople, whom he likewise makes witnesses, giving them a sense of faith and of grace.[49]

Christ entrusted the Scriptures and the understanding of them to the entire Church, and the hierarchy has no mission to silence the faithful. On the contrary, the role of the hierarchy is to stir up the charisms and keep them alive: "Do not stifle the Spirit. Do not despise the gift of prophecy. Test everything; retain what is good."[50] It would be false to claim that until now the Christian people has never exercised its prophetic gift and that since Vatican II, all of a sudden, that people has become wise. History before the Council cries otherwise to us. The great movements that have flowered, like a series of springs in the Church, and which have brightened and warmed its sometimes difficult journey in the midst of the world, and that, it must be said, were in part responsible for Vatican II itself—I am thinking of the biblical and liturgical movements, and of Catholic Action—all these started among the people, and did not owe their existence to the hierarchy. When they succeeded, the hierarchy blessed them. But it did not initiate them. This was not its role. But it did authenticate them. However, the people's exercise of its prophetic mission took place outside the celebration of the liturgy. At the door of the church the laity became dumb; the only right they had was to say "Amen." One dug a moat, separating life and liturgy, prophetism and cult. Today, this moat is slowly being filled in. "A tranquil revolution among Catholics"[51] has occurred: they are taking ownership of their liturgy. Even the notion of "active participation," so dear to Vatican II, is insufficient.[52] For it is not a part, however large or small, that belongs to the people of God. The celebration in its integrity belongs to them, to each celebrant according to their place and charism in the Church.

In countries long Christian and in North America, certain communities have made immense efforts in the formation of lay people. They have full access to the sources of knowledge. Thus they enrich the entire Church. They will not resign themselves any longer to being dispossessed of prophetic charism. They are fully ready to take the homily in charge. They are doing this in the case of Sun-

---

[49] *Lumen Gentium*, 35.
[50] 1 Thess 5:19-21.
[51] This is the title of the book by M. Hébrard, Éd. du Centurion, Paris, 1989.
[52] P.-M. Gy, "Liturgie" in *Dictionnaire de Spiritualité*, Vol. 9, 1976, col. 911.

day celebrations in the absence of a priest, and often they do it admirably.

The situation is different in certain Third World countries or in mission countries.[53] Small base communities are the most numerous here. The lack of priests is the general rule; certain central missions are surrounded by a circle of more than a hundred small communities. These little communities are also the poorest. They only receive a priestly visit once or twice a year. Their understanding of the Word is not founded on the same intellectual base as ours. But who dare suggest that it is less profound? Understanding of the mystery of God mocks simple human intelligence. Is not the Father in heaven pleased to reveal his mystery to the little ones? Does he not cherish a preferential love for the poorest? These communities which gather together a fistful of faithful in the African brush, or in the anonymity of a town of the Third World, are the roots which make the Church grow and blossom.

A member of the faithful discovers during a passing visit to the central mission the God of tenderness, the Father of our Lord Jesus Christ. Wonder seizes his heart. He returns to his animist village. No one told him to gather his friends, but he does it. No one told him to teach them to pray, but he prays with them. No one deputed him to give the homily, he does not even know the definition of a homily, yet he gives it admirably. He escapes the gaze of canon law, but not the gaze of God. The Spirit inhabits his word.

What is the role of the presider, the one mandated by authority to preside at the celebration? The role is to authenticate the Word which is pronounced under his responsibility. He affirms by his presence that this Word conforms to the teaching of the Church, that the faithful may receive it as the rule of faith. He completes the homily if he judges it opportune. He corrects it if he judges it necessary. He approves it, sometimes simply by his silence, for silence in the case where one ought to speak is approbation. His responsibility remains entire, whether he gives the homily himself, or whether he allows someone else to give it.

Let us add that at a certain level the homily is everyone's business. Those who are ministers of the Word do what they can; some

[53] "In 1963 half of all Catholics still lived in Europe and North America. In the year 2000, there will not be more than 30 percent" (A. Peelman, *L'inculturation et les cultures*, Desclée, Paris, 1988, 20). This is to realize the importance of the Third World for the future of Christianity.

days, as they are well aware, their homily never quite gets off the ground, and they are the first to acknowledge it. They also know that to give a good homily is a grace from the Spirit. Those who listen must also do what they can. There is a threshold in the consciousness of the hearers that no one can cross but themselves. It is the threshold beyond which the noise of human words has stopped and each individual must say: "Speak Lord, your servant is listening." Thus there is a homily which no one else can preach in our stead. It is a homily we must listen to in silent adoration.

If those who give the homily must prepare themselves seriously in order to speak according to the Spirit of God, those who listen must also prepare themselves to receive according to the same Spirit. Chrysostom (407) gives a wise counsel when he begins one of his homilies thus:

> Before coming to the words of the Gospel I have a favor to ask you. I shall ask of you nothing hard or heavy. If you agree, it will be useful not only for me, but especially for you who accord to my request. What is therefore my request?
>
> That the first day of the week, or even on Saturday, each of you take up the passage of the Gospel which will be read during the assembly (the following Sunday). That you explore and examine what is said. That you note what is clear, what is obscure, what appears contradictory, even if it is not truly contradictory. Thus you will come to the assembly after having reflected well about everything.
>
> It will not be a skimpy profit that we shall receive together from this study. For us, we shall no longer have to take so much trouble to explain to you the sense of the words, since your spirit will already be accustomed to what is said. And you yourselves will listen and learn with a more penetrating and perspicacious spirit.[54]

HOMILY AND PRAYER

It would be stating a foregone conclusion to affirm the necessity of prayer to the Spirit of Jesus in order to understand the words inspired by the Spirit and to explain them correctly to the community. It is the Spirit who leads us to "the entire truth."[55] Prayer is the path to God. Origen (†253–254) counsels his former pupil Gregory the Wonderworker:

[54] *Homilies on John*, homily 11.1. — PG 59, 77.
[55] John 16:13.

In applying yourself to this divine reading, seek with uprightness and with an unshakeable confidence in God the sense of the divine Writings, hidden to the multitude. Do not be content to knock and to seek, for it is absolutely necessary to pray in order to understand divine things.[56]

Origen concludes the beginning of his commentary on John's Gospel:

It is time to ask God to help us through Christ in the Holy Spirit to discover the mystical sense as a treasure under the words.[57]

"It is time to ask God . . . ." It is always time to ask God from the moment one enters into the garden of the divine Scriptures. One of the principles of ancient exegesis may be formulated thus: the same grace is necessary to understand the Word of God as is necessary for offering it and explaining it. In his *Discourse of Thanks to Origen*, Gregory the Wonderworker explains:

All he [Origen] says has no other source in my opinion than a communication of the divine Spirit: the same power is necessary to those who prophesy and to those who listen to the prophets; and none may listen to a prophet if the Spirit who has prophesied in the prophet does not give them the understanding of the words.[58]

Without doubt the proposition is a little excessive. In strict theology the charism of giving prophecy must not be confused with the charism of interpreting it. Yet it expresses well the difficulty of understanding the Word without the grace of the Spirit. The recommendation, which the ancient Jewish tradition addressed to speakers who were asking themselves what they were going to say to the community (and which of us has never experienced this panic before speaking?), is still true today: "You will learn from God."[59]

The homily is born of prayer. In a certain sense it is prayer itself. If prayer is the dialogue between God and us; if the essential of this dialogue does not consist so much in recounting our lives to God—which he knows about anyway, better than we do and before we do—but first of all making room in our hearts for silence in order to listen to him, then the welcoming of the Word

[56] *Lettre d'Origène à Grégoire le Thaumaturge*, 4, Trad. H. Crouzel, SC, 148, 1969, 193, 195.
[57] *Commentaire sur saint Jean*, I, 89 Trad. C. Blanc, SC, 120, 1966, 105.
[58] *Remerciement à Origène*, 15. Trad. H. Crouzel, SC, 148, 1969, 171.
[59] Strack-Billerbeck, vol. IV, *op. cit.*, 172.

is Christian prayer par excellence. And if the homily is the actualization of this Word, then it too is the actualization of this prayer. The homily lives in prayer as a bird lives in the sky. It is always listening to God, praising God's holy will and love, asking for God's grace. Origen does not hesitate to interrupt his explanation of the sacred text with the following prayer:

> It is the Lord himself, it is the Holy Spirit whom we must implore. May the Spirit dispel every cloud and every obscurity which, because of the impurity of our sins darken what is in our heart. May we seize upon the spiritual and wonderful understanding of his Law, like the psalmist who said: "Open my eyes that I may see the wonders of your Law."[60]

One of these homilies finishes with this ardent prayer:

> Let us pray to the Lord . . . That we may consider in the Spirit what has been written by the Spirit. That we may explain the texts in a manner worthy of God and of the Holy Spirit who has inspired them in Christ, our Savior. To him be the glory and the power for ever and ever. Amen.[61]

This doxology is the usual way Origen concludes his homilies. Thus, the thirty-nine homilies on Luke's Gospel dating from the years 248–249, which the tradition has conserved for us, all conclude with the doxology (borrowed from 1 Pet 4:11): "To Christ be the glory and the power for ever and ever. Amen." Here is a particularly beautiful conclusion:

> Let us stand together. In the place of Israel in the flesh, let us become the spiritual Israel. Let us bless Almighty God, in work, in thought and in word, in Christ Jesus. To him be the glory and the power for ever and ever. Amen.[62]

What might have appeared only as a discourse on Scripture has become praise of Christ; the explanation of the Word has been transfigured into adoration; actualization has become glorification of God.

---

[60] *Homélies sur le Lévitique*, I, 1. — Cf. *SC*, 286, 1982, 70. See A. Hamman, *La Prière*, vol. II, Desclée, Paris, 1963, 318–323 ("De la prédication à la prière").
[61] *Homélies sur les Nombres*, XVI, 9. Cf. *SC*, 29, 1951, 336.
[62] *Homélies sur saint Luc*, XII, 6. — Cf. *SC*, 87, 1962, 204.

THE VOCATION OF THE PREACHER

Preachers must be "faithful dispensers of the Word of truth."[63] May Christ, on the last day, recognize as his own each word that we have pronounced in his name! Humility is required for this ministry. Humility before the Word itself: "There are too many mysteries in the scriptures."[64] In addition, there is too much darkness in our spirits. The one who would yield to vanity and preach a showy homily would be "a fraudulant trafficker of the Word."[65]

Humility before the community is also essential. Anyone who accepts the ministry of presenting the Word also accepts the obligation of being the first to listen to the Word. They must humbly gauge the abyss between the message they proclaim and the manner in which they live it. "I know my soul, its greatness and its littleness," said John Chrysostom (†407), "I know the greatness of this service and the difficulty of this ministry."[66] The *Didache* says that "every prophet who teaches the truth without putting it into practice is a false prophet."[67] Theologically, one can criticize this statement, since the Church must practice what it teaches. It would be reduced to teaching very little if it had to be perfectly holy before it spoke. It would have remained silent since the very first day. Preaching is a school of humility. The gold of the Gospel is carried in an earthen vessel.[68] Is the vessel to preen itself because of its gold?

Here we see the paradox of preaching: one proclaims salvation to the world but carries the burden of one's own wretchedness. Preacher of God's freely given mercy, one must first implore it for oneself. One speaks with authority and has yet no authority over the message one transmits. One is only a steward, yet it is the very treasures of God that one's lips reveal to the world! We are "ambassadors for Christ, God himself, appealing through us."[69]

---

[63] 2 Tim 2:15.
[64] Pamphilius, *Origen's Apology*, PG 17, 543.
[65] 1 Cor 2:17.
[66] *Sur le sacerdoce*, III, 7. SC, 272, 1980, 159.
[67] *Didachè*, 11, 10. — Cf. SC, 248, 1978, 186.
[68] Cf. 2 Cor 4:7.
[69] 2 Cor 5:20.

5
The Prayer of the Faithful

THE LESSON OF THE PAST

The Constitution of the Sacred Liturgy of 1963 decided to restore the ancient "common prayer or prayer of the faithful" (*oratio communis seu fidelium* 153).

The General Instruction on the Roman Missal, 45 (*Institutio generalis missalis romani*) of 1969, citing the Constitution on the Liturgy, brought this restoration to fruition. The GIRM modified the terminology. The "common prayer" is to be called from now on "universal prayer." It also keeps the title "prayer of the faithful." One therefore has the choice of two titles: "universal prayer" or "prayer of the faithful."

In regard to liturgical history, the title "prayer of the faithful" recalls that this prayer was prayed formerly once the catechumens and the penitents had been sent out of the assembly, and only the faithful remained. The GIRM keeps this title and gives it a beautiful significance: "In the universal prayer or prayer of the faithful, the people, exercising their priestly function, intercedes for all humanity." We have here without doubt the best definition of the universal prayer.

Certain authors, in order to underline the universality of Christian intercession, avoid the term "prayer of the faithful" and prefer to speak solely of the "universal prayer."[1]

---

[1] P. de Clerck, La *"Prière universelle" dans les liturgies latines anciennes*, coll. "Liturgiewissenschaftliche Quellen und Forschungen," 62, 1977, 308–310 (one finds in this book the best study of the universal prayer in the Latin tradition).
See also the remarks of P.-M. Gy in *La Maison-Dieu*, 129, 1977, 150.

The *Ordo Lectionum*, 30 (1981) keeps the two titles and suggests that in a certain way that this prayer may be said to respond to the Word of God that has just been proclaimed.

There is therefore a certain problem of vocabulary, but not such as to let loose a war of words. The essential lies in the reality of this prayer. Such reality, like all prayer, is marvellous. It entrusts intercession for the whole world to the humblest of Christians in our liturgical assemblies.

Tradition has given us a text from the First Letter of Timothy as the scriptural basis for the universal prayer:

> I recommend that before all else, that petitions, prayers, intercessions, thanksgivings be made for all people; for kings and for those in authority, so that we may lead calm and peaceable lives, in all piety and dignity. This is what pleases God our Savior, he who wishes all people to be saved and to come to the knowledge of the truth (1 Tim 2:1-4).

This text strongly affirms the universality of Christian prayer: it is made "for all people." It joins itself to the will of God that desires that "all people should be saved." It prolongs the Jewish tradition in its intercession for those who hold authority.[2] It echoes the teaching of Jesus who demands of his disciples to pray even for their enemies and their persecutors, so to become children of the heavenly Father "who makes his sun rise on the good and on the wicked and who makes rain fall on the just and on the injust.[3]

This text of 1 Timothy 2.1-4 does not explain the universal prayer of the present-day Mass.[4] It simply shows that it fits well into the scriptural tradition.

The first explicit witness to the universal prayer is found in Justin (†c.165), in his *First Apology* (drawn up about 150). He describes the prayer which takes place just before the Eucharist properly speaking of a Baptismal Mass:

---

[2] C. Spicq, *Les Épîtres Pastorales*, coll. Études Bibliques," 1969, 360.

[3] Matt 5:45.

[4] We do not know the date of this text, for we are not sure of its Pauline authenticity; the date given varies according to authors, between 65 and the beginning of the second century. S. De Lestapis, who defends the integral Pauline authenticity of the Pastorals, even proposes 58 for the date of 1 Tim. (*L'énigme des Pastorales de Saint Paul*, Gabalda, Paris, 1976, 304. We also do not know what the structure of the Mass was at that time.

We pray together with fervor for ourselves, for the one who has just been enlightened [baptized], for everyone else, in whatever place they find themselves, so as to be judged worthy, after having learnt the truth, to practice good works, to keep the commandments and to thus obtain eternal salvation (*Apology* I. 65).

He then describes the Sunday Mass:

On the day called day of the sun, all, whether they live in the town or in the country, gather together in the same place.
(*Reading of the Word*)
Then the Memoirs of the Apostles are read [the Gospels] or the Writings of the Prophets, for as long as time allows.
(*Homily*)
When the reader has finished, the one who presides takes up the Word and exhorts the assembly to imitate its worthy teachings.
(*Universal Prayer*)
We then stand all together and we pray.
(*Celebration of the Eucharist*)
Then, as we have said above, when the prayer is finished, bread and wine and water are brought. The one who presides offers prayers and thanksgivings for as long as he is able, and all the people respond by the acclamation: Amen (*Apology* I.67).

The witness of Justin allows us to conclude that a prayer existed which was placed after the readings and before the bread and wine was brought up. We also know what the intentions of this prayer were; one prayed for the community, for the neophytes, for the faithful of the whole world.

Following Justin, we know numerous litany prayers. They are proliferated especially in the Eastern liturgies, sometimes excessively, at least for our Western piety.[5] But even the story of the universal prayer properly speaking loses itself in the paths of numerous Eastern and Western liturgies. Paul de Clerck judged with a wise prudence: "Yes, the primitive Church knew of the universal prayer, but perhaps not everywhere, nor at its origins, nor during the whole of

---

[5] Thus the *Apostolic Constitutions* (about 380) present a litanic prayer for the catechumens, another for the faithful, and, after the Consecration, a litanic prayer of the bishop and another of the deacon (see L. Deiss *Springtime of the Liturgy*. Collegeville: The Liturgical Press). We know that the multiplication of prayers is sometimes the cause of their devaluation.

the first five centuries. It probably owes its origins more to the order given by 1 Timothy 2:1-2 than to influences from the Jewish liturgy."[6]

Concerning the Church of Rome, one may cite the solemn prayers of Good Friday (prayers which were originally made up of invitatories alone) between about 250 and 320. Pope Gelasius (492–496) is credited with the introduction of a litany prayer into the Roman liturgy. This prayer, commonly called *Deprecatio papae Gelasii*, sometimes had *Kyrie eleison* as the response. It existed until the middle of the sixth century, then disappeared.

We are ignorant of the link which may have existed between the universal prayer and the *Kyrie* at the beginning of Mass, as also with the intercessions that are found again after the Consecration in the Eucharistic Prayers. Traces of the universal prayer are found in the last part of the Litany of the Saints, as well as in the prayers of the prône which had a dialogue form until the fifteenth century.[7]

The restoration of the universal prayer is one of the greatest successes of Vatican II. R. Cabie presents the situation well: "The universal prayer appears as the climax of the whole Liturgy of the Word and as the threshold of the Eucharist properly speaking. Placed after the dismissal of the catechumens, it is the privilege of the faithful, which underlines its priestly character. We may say that it is the other face of evangelization, to speak about people to God may not be disassociated with speaking of God to people."[8]

THE DUTY OF THE PRESENT

In the celebration of the liturgy, the universal prayer is organically linked to the celebration of the Word. It lifts up its voice while the voice of God is still resounding in the assembly. This is the normal rhythm of prayer:

• God speaks to human beings, revealing to them his mystery.
• Human beings respond to God in opening their hearts to him.

---

[6] P. de Clerck, *op. cit.*, 110.

[7] Certain German speaking dioceses knew Common prayer or intercessions which were recited at all Masses after the Gospel or the homily (see J. Gülden, W. Muschick, *Fürbitten*, Christophorus-Verlag, Freiburg im Breisgau, 1965, 5).

[8] R. Cabié, *The Church at Prayer*, vol II, Collegeville, The Liturgical Press, 1979, 1986.

It is not the only response to the Word of God. The essential response to the Word is the celebration of the Eucharist strictly speaking. It is a response of praise, of blessing, of thanksgiving that is linked directly to the Word that, according to the teaching of Vatican II, "the two parts, the liturgy of the Word and the liturgy of the Eucharist . . . constitute one single act of worship."⁹ This single act of worship is the celebration of the Covenant (cf. 45–54). Yet the universal prayer presents this response in the form of petition, in the cadre of the Mass. It may also present it in the form of thanksgiving in Sunday assemblies in the absence of a priest.

Let us underline here two qualities of the universal prayer: its biblical nature and its universality.

A biblical prayer

In speaking of the biblical character of the universal prayer, the petitions of this prayer are generally rooted in the Word that has just been celebrated, so that we celebrate the Word under the form of petitions. In a certain sense, the community is "sown" with the Word. This seed springs up in the form of prayer.

This rooting of the universal prayer in the Word has not been received universally with the same conviction. Certain authors think that this prayer must keep its autonomy. In analizing the most ancient prayer formulas they think that they had no link with the readings that preceded them. One may judge that it is without doubt the fixity of the formulas that explains the absence of a link: one does not change traditional formulas, especially if they are good literary pieces. We may also think that it is without doubt the fixity of the formulas that explains the rapid decline of the universal prayer, then its disappearance in the sixth century from the Roman liturgy.

Yet it is permissible to think that the past history of the universal prayer does not have to be the sole criterion, still less the absolute criterion, for the present liturgy. If the homily is the actualization of the Word of God, the universal prayer is also fully concerned with this actualization. The *Ordo Lectionum*, 30, makes a remark which makes good liturgical sense:

⁹ *Sacrosanctum Concilium*, 55.

Enlightened by God's Word and in a sense responding to it, the assembly of the faithful prays in the general intercessions. . . .[10]

As an example, let us suppose that the Gospel cites the word of Jesus in his inaugural sermon: "Be merciful as your heavenly Father is merciful."[11] If the homily affirms that "today this Word is accomplished for us, today the Lord asks us to be merciful as the heavenly father is merciful," how could the universal prayer not link itself to the Word by the petition: "Give us the grace to be merciful as your Son Jesus asks of us today"?

Our prayer always has need of being evangelized. It must be in accord with the heart of God in such a way that the Holy Spirit, who is the soul of our prayer, may make the words of our heart her own. It will be all the more deeply this if it reflects the Word that has given it birth.

The four series of intentions

The Constitution on the Liturgy suggests four series of intentions. The universal prayer intercedes:

• for the Church.
• for those in authority.
• for those who are burdened with various necessities.
• for all people and for the salvation of the whole world (53).

These four series of intentions may be regarded as a "cadre of the law"[12] in which the community expresses itself with a "wise liberty" (*sapienti libertate*) as the *Ordo Lectionum* remarks.

This cadre of the law reminds each community that it must be open to the needs of the universal Church. It intends to stimulate creativity, not to stifle it. The universal prayer will be saved from the routine of repetitive formulas if it roots itself in the Word of God. Just as the Word is renewed each day, just as the homily discovers new horizons each day in actualizing this Word, so too the universal prayer, rooted in the ground of the Word, flowers each day in new intentions inspired by the Spirit of God.

[10] OLM, 30. See however the remarks of P. De Clerck in *La Maison-Dieu* 153, 1983, which make precise the limits of this affirmation.
[11] Luke 6:36.
[12] See our remarks in *Concile et chant nouveau*, Éd. du Levain, Paris, 1968, 191.

Communities omit the universal prayer because they are tired
of repeating the four intentions at each Mass ("Let us pray for the
Church, for those who govern us, for the poor, for the salvation
of the world"). They should, however, be renewing themselves in
a prayer inspired by the Word. The particular intentions which are
proposed must be accepted with goodwill, even if they sometimes
have no link with the four series of "official" intentions nor with
the readings which precede them. These intentions may make mention of diverse simple happenings in the local district, or in the local streets, for the most insignificant happening may become the
occasion for lifting up one's face to God. There is a certain grandeur in this way of praying, while at the same time a certain pettiness. The grandeur is confidence in God. We know that God's ear
is sensitive, so sensitive that he discerns in the most banal intentions the heart which cries out to God, amidst the universal tumult,
the smallest lament of those who scarcely dare murmur their sor-
row and who hide their face. Yet there is also a certain pettiness
on our part: that of mixing up the God of supreme glory with our
little human histories. The most astonishing thing is that this "works"
and that God in infinite tenderness also hears these miserable
prayers:

> The Lord is close to those who call upon him,
> to all those who call upon him in truth! (Ps 145:18)

It suffices to present ourselves with our pain before the Lord,
and he bends his face towards us. This is what Ezekiel did in the
time of the prophet Isaiah. When he received the letter of Sen-
nacherib, which announced that the Assyrians were going to burn
Jerusalem and put its inhabitants to the sword, he went to the
Temple, unfolded the letter before Yahweh, and said: "Yahweh,
open your eyes and see!"[13] This is what each community must do:
present itself before the Lord, show him its heart and say to him:
"Lord, open your eyes and see!"

A universal prayer

The prayer of the Catholic Church is universal by definition
(*katholicos*, in classical Greek, signifies "universal"). If not, it de-

---

[13] 2 Kgs 19:16.

generates and degrades itself as the prayer of a sect. It is catholic not only because it intercedes for all people, but even more because it intercedes in the name of all people.[14] The liturgy teaches us to pray in the plural. No one has the right to say "My Father in heaven, give me this day my daily bread." No one, except Christ who alone was able to say in all truth: "My Father and your Father."[15] Prayer, contemplation of God, also looks upon the human family; it is a remembrance of all humanity. It is universal because it is exactly the part that each community, even the humblest, takes in the immense distress as well as the profound joy of all people.

Vatican II affirms that each particular Church must "represent as perfectly as possible the universal Church."[16] It is on this particular Church, even if it is reduced to a few members of the faithful, that the future of the Church rests, the fate of the whole of humanity. The particular Church intercedes before God for billions of human beings. Between God and the nations, God has placed this Christian community. Between God and the suffering of the world, God has placed the intercession of this community.

Particular intentions

It is normal that this prayer, since it is universal, welcomes equally particular intentions and offers moments of silence. Neither the "official" intentions nor the biblical intentions meet all the needs of the community. Certain intentions cannot be presented publicly. One carries them like a joyful treasure, a ray of light, a weight which weighs on the heart. A time of silence where all present their thoughts before God is always welcome. Sometimes one may reproach celebrations for being too wordy, for devouring the silence by filling it with words. Such a reproach cannot be made to well-structured celebrations that know how to accommodate moments of recollection in the midst of prayer.

Anaphoric Intercessions

Anaphoric intercessions are those intercessions that one finds in the anaphoras (Eucharistic Prayers) after the Consecration.

---

[14] "The people, exercizing their priestly function, intercede for all people," GIRM, 45.
[15] John 20:17.
[16] *Ad Gentes*, 20.

The ancient Jewish blessings, which have no doubt served as patterns for our Eucharistic Prayers, regularly conclude with petitions. This is a normal movement in prayer: after having lifted one's hands to bless God, one holds them out to him in petition. These petitions are in our present anaphoras. Thus in Eucharistic Prayer 4 we pray for the pope, for the bishops, for priests, for all people who seek God with sincerity, for the dead, for the celebrating community. The Coptic liturgy, for example, prays for needs in detail: for the seeds during the season of sowing (from October 7 to January 5), for the fruits during the season of fruits (from January 6 to June 6), for a good overflow of the Nile (from June 7 to October 6).

However venerable they are, these prayers risk slowing down the natural movement of thanksgiving. They also risk appearing as repeats of the universal prayer. Such repeating will be less weighty if the universal prayer is rooted in the Word of God.[17]

[17] P. de Clerck notes: "It is inevitable that the evolution of these three similar elements: penitential litany, universal prayer and anaphoric intercessions, provoke objections and that in the future mutations and readjustments will happen" (in *La Maison-Dieu* 153, 1983, 131).

6
The Actors in the Celebration

We shall consider here the actors in the celebration: the assembly itself, its presider, and the readers.

THE ASSEMBLY

In the past popular language affirmed that the priest "celebrated" the Mass and that the people "assisted." There was no theological intent in this way of speaking, still less an animosity toward the clergy. It simply reflected the sensibility of the Christian people. This vision of liturgy was also well manifested in the architecture of certain churches: a raised sanctuary, of unequal proportion in regard to the rest of the church, well separated from the nave, gave the impression of being the stage on which the "actors" played their roles: the nave seemed like the part of the theater where the audience sat. As for the choir, just as in certain operas, it was outside the audience's field of vision, in the choir loft. This arrangement focused on the specificity of the ordained ministry. It also manifested the distance which separated the Christian people from its liturgy and the liturgy from their lives. And if one had asked: "Who celebrates the liturgy of the Word?" the reply would have been: "The priest." Besides, he read the texts in Latin, without even addressing the people.

Vatican II restored the early Christian biblical theology according to which the whole Church is a priestly people. Even if the Church is structured in an organic manner as people with ministers at their service, as flock and shepherd, as lay people on the one hand, and bishops, priests, and deacons on the other, it is still the whole assembly which is the celebrant. Each member of the faithful, from the smallest infant to the bishop, concelebrates, each one according to his or her place.[1] The Council presents this theology of concelebration as follows:

> Liturgical actions are the celebrations of the Church which is the sacrament of unity. . . . That is why they belong to the whole Body of the Church, they manifest it and they affect it.[2]

Each baptized person may therefore be called a "celebrant." The vocabulary itself of the official texts has evolved on this point.[3] Thus the first edition of the GIRM, of 1969, spoke of the priest as "celebrant." This was changed in the following edition of 1970, which spoke of the "priest celebrant" (*sacerdos celebrans*[4]) in order to signify that all the faithful are "celebrants."

This theological vision, which had been covered by the dust of centuries of liturgical nonchalance and which Vatican II "dusted" with vigor, allows us to respond to the question: "Who are the actors in the celebration of the Word?" "The whole celebating community." A single reader proclaims the text, but the whole celebrating community receives it as the Word of God. A single person gives the homily, but the whole celebrating community actualizes the Word of God. A single person speaks the universal prayer, but the whole celebrating community intercedes.

THE PRESIDER

In speaking of "the one who presides at the liturgy of the Word" (*qui liturgiae Verbi praeest*), the *Ordo Lectionum* 38-43 avoids the

---

[1] See M.-J. Congar, "L'Ecclesia ou communauté chrétienne, sujet intégral de l'action liturgique," in *Vatican II*, coll. *Unam Sanctam*, 66, 241–282.

[2] *Sacrosanctum Concilium*, 26.

[3] See the remarks of C. Pottie and D. Lebrun, "La doctrine de l'Ecclesia, sujet intégral de la célébration dans les livres liturgiques depuis Vatican II," in *La Maison-Dieu*, 176, 1989, 177–132.

[4] GIRM, 34, 42, 244, 248.

word "priest." In assemblies in mission countries and in certain communities of countries long Christian, the presider may be assumed
by a deacon or a layperson.

Yet it is evident that the priest, when he presides, bears a particular responsibility for the Word. Vatican II affirms:

> The people of God is gathered together first of all by the Word
> of God, which it is most fitting to hear from the mouths of
> priests. . . . The first function of the priest is to announce the Gospel
> of God to all people.[5]
> They are consecrated in order to preach the Gospel.[6]

What is said of the presider is said therefore of whoever assumes
this ministry, and especially of the priest. The presider bears before God the responsibility for the celebration of the Word.

It is not required that he gives the introductions to the readings
himself, introductions which give useful keys to understanding the
Word. But he bears responsibility for these introductions.

It is not required that he reads the readings himself. It is al-
together preferable that he entrusts them to the readers. But he bears
the responsibility for the readings. If the Word is disfigured by an
unworthy reading, he carries the responsibility before God.

It is not required that he gives the homily himself. He may share
it with others. But if it wanders off in the swamp of political or
worldly discourse, he has the duty to bring it back to the path of
the Gospel: he gives the homily. To preside over the homily in this
way can be more exacting than to do it himself. It is always easier
to say a right word than to redress a wrong one.

It is not required that he pray the universal prayer himself. But
if this prayer neglects the intentions of the universal Church, if it
is only a narcissistic contemplation of the miseries of the community, he bears the responsibility. And if it opens itself with charity
to the distress of the world, his is the merit, along with his community, before God.

In brief, he may delegate all that is in his power, save one thing:
his own responsibility. This is to lead the community to respond
to the Word in "listening and adoration in Spirit and in truth.[7]

---

[5] *Presbyterorum ordinis,* 4.
[6] *Lumen Gentium,* 28. See also *Dei Verbum,* 25.
[7] *OLM,* 6, citing John 4:23.

To serve the community

To preside is not to dominate. It is simply to render a hierarchical service. To preside in the community is to serve the community.

This service will be so much the more accepted by the community if the presider gives an example. When the community is engaged in the penitential preparation at the beginning of Mass, may the presider be the first to recognize himself as a sinner and implore forgiveness. When it listens to the Word, may he be the first to listen. When it actualizes the homily, may he be the first to put this actualization into practice. When it responds in the universal prayer, may he be the first to intercede.

There is no domination in this service. It is simply a greater invitation to imitate Christ Jesus. Blessed be the presider—be they bishop, priest, deacon or lay person—who can say to the community with Christ Jesus: "I am among you as one who serves."[8]

THE READER

What is the exact ministerial function of the reader?

It is simple to understand, more difficult to realize, seldom attained with perfection: it is the proclaim the Word of God to the celebrating community in a fully intelligible manner, with "clarity and wisdom," as the *Ordo Lectionum* 14 says. The ministry of reader is not therefore first of all to read the text, but, in reading it, to make it understood. Who would dare affirm that the readings read in our assemblies are always perfectly understood? In the voice of the reader, we must hear the clear voice of Christ. For, as Vatican II affirms, it is he, Christ, "who speaks when the holy Scriptures are read in the Church."[9]

Christian tradition entrusted this ministry to members of the faithful who had confessed their faith during the persecutions. Cyprian of Carthage (†258) explained:

---

[8] Luke 22:27.
[9] *Sacrosanctum Concilium*, 7. On the reader, see the fine text of the Spanish episcopal commission in *Notitiae*, 228–229 (1985), 422–444 (with bibliography).

Nothing is more fitting to the voice which has confessed God by a glorious witness, than to be heard in the divine readings. . . to read the Gospel of Christ which made the martyrs, and to come to the ambo after having been at the pillory.[10]

Do our readers today realize that they are the successors of the martyrs and that their voice must be as convincing as the voice of blood?

Who may assume the ministry of reader?

Certain authors assume that in the office of the synagogue, "one had the right, in the beginning, to call no matter who, women, children, and even slaves included, to read the Torah."[11] The historian Flavius Josephus († after 95) affirms, not without a certain boastfulness, that the children knew how to recite the Law better than to say their own name.[12] Without doubt, one must not generalize certain affirmations, for situations may be different for different communities and for different eras. That the possibility of calling women to read the reading was abolished from the period of the Tannaim[13] is accepted (this period extended from the foundation of the school of Jamnia after A.D. 70 to the third century).

It is interesting to note a certain fluctuation in the practice of the apostolic communities. In his First Letter to the Corinthians, in about the year 54, Paul allows women to intervene in the celebrations. He writes: "Every man who prays and prophesizes. . . . ," and "every women who prays and prophesizes . . . . "[14] He thus affirms the perfect equality of man and woman. The woman, like the man, may pray and prophesy, thus may speak and teach in the name of the Holy Spirit. This disposition reflects well the Pauline principle of the letter to the Galatians (from the same era as the first letter to the Corinthians): in Christ Jesus, "there is neither Jew

---

[10] Epistula 38:2. Cf. *Saint-Cyprien. Correspondence*, coll. des Universités de France, Budé, Société d'Édition "Les Belles Lettres," 1925, 96.

[11] I. Elbogen, *Der Jüdische Gottesdienst in seiner Geschichtlichen Entwicklung,* OLMS, Hildesheim, 1962, 170.

[12] *Contre Apion, XVIII.* Coll. des Universités de France, *Société d'Édition* "Les Belles Lettres," 1972, 89.

[13] Cf. Strack-Billerbeck, *Kommentar zum Neuen Testament aus Talmud und Midrasch,* Éd. C. H. Bek, München, vol. IV, 1961, 157–158.

[14] 1 Cor 11:4-5.

nor Greek, slave nor free, man nor woman"[15] (Gal 3:28). But another text suppresses this equality and gives a new rule: "Let women keep quiet in the assemblies, for it is not permitted to them to speak. . . . If they wish to understand some point, let them ask their husbands at home."[16] And those who were not married, whom do they ask?[17] Has Paul let himself be influenced here by his former rabbinic background? Or was this text later introduced into Paul's letter by Judeo-Christian integrists?[18] It echoes another text which is of a much later date, namely, the First Letter of Timothy (2:11-12):

> During instruction, women must be silent.
> I do not allow a woman to teach.[19]

The reform of new liturgy has likewise raised certain clouds in the sky of the new liturgy. The first edition of the new missal, promulgated with the authorization of episcopal conferences, did not allow women to read, "except in the absence of a man apt to exercize the function of reader."[20] This seemed to prefer an unworthy reading to a women reading clearly. In addition, such a women reader had to read from "outside the sanctuary." But these dispositions were so contrary both to the sensibilities of communities and to what was already being practiced universally, that they fell into oblivion in the second edition: the discriminatory paragraph was simply omitted.

It seems to me that the rule conforms to good sense—and good sense is the first of Christian rubrics: the ministry of reader is a service of the Word of God for the benefit of the celebrating community. Let us choose for this service the one who can best assure it for the community. If this is a man, let us choose this man. If it is a woman, let us choose this woman. If it is a boy or a girl, let us choose this boy or this girl.

---

[15] Gal 3:28.

[16] 1 Cor 14:34.

[17] There existed in the Corinthian community a group of "virgins" (1 Cor 7:25).

[18] See J.-M. Aubert, L'exil féminin, Éd. du Cerf, Paris, 1988, 54–59. C. Senet, La première Épître de saint Paul aux Corinthiens, Ed. Delachaux et Niestlé, Neuchâtel-Paris, 182–183.

[19] 1 Tim 2:11-12. The majority of exegetes (90 percent after R. E. Brown, The Churches the Apostles Left Behind, Paulist Press, New York, 1979) think that the Pastorals are deutero-Pauline. They were not, then, written—at least in their integrity—by Paul himself.

[20] GIRM, 66.

This "rule" does not require that we alternate male and female, young and old, at the ambo. It does not prevent it either. It simply affirms that alternation is not the question. For the aim of the readings has nothing to do with the alternation of the readers. There is a single goal to be achieved, on the one hand, of the Word: that it be read as well as possible; and on the other hand, of the community: that it receive the Word as well as possible.

Number of readings

According to the ancient traditon of the synagogal liturgy, the reading of the Word was assured by three readers in ordinary celebrations and by as many as seven readers on the Sabbath and on feast days.[21] This arrangement signified that no one had a monopoly over the Word. It is the entire community that possesses this treasure and that shares it.

This plurality of readers is desirable today. The *Ordo Lectionum* (52), strongly recommends it. One must not see the same reader read the first reading, then the Psalm, then the second reading, and sometimes even the Alleluia verse, reducing all the greyness of a monotone recitation. Giving each reading a different reader with a different face and a particular voice, renews the attention of the community. One also discreetly underlines the specificity of each reading.

Indispensable technique

To know how to read is not sufficient. It is a question of entering into communication with an assembly and of making the text understood, sometimes of speaking into a microphone which is badly regulated or with which one needs to regulate one's voice, in a church where reverberation may drown the most eloquent elocution with loud music. All this, without counting the fact that certain texts are not immediately accessible nor easily understood. One has only to think of certain of Paul's flights against the Jewish integrists! It is therefore with reason that the introduction to the Missal and the introduction to the Lectionary recommends:

[21] Megillah, 4:1-2. Cf. H. Danby, *The Mishna*, Clarendon Press, Oxford, 1933, 205-206.

A technical preparation should make the readers more skilled in the art of reading publicly, either with the power of their own voice or with the help of sound equipment.[22]

In the area of technique, there are no miracles. The generosity of volunteers, even their holiness, cannot make up for a microphone that hisses or a voice which mumbles. "A donkey plunged in holy water," said the mystic Toukaram, (†1650) "does not come out as a pure bred."[23] The holy man was right. To assume this ministry without preparation is to tempt providence.

At a time when radio and television sometimes give us such excellent examples of technique, it would be intolerable for the children of light to be content with makeshift in this area, and to show themselves less able than those in show business.

Necessary preparation

The reader needs to be familiar with the text to be read. To take a volunteer at the last minute at the beginning of Mass and to ask: "Is there anyone who would like to do the reading?" is to give proof of a disregard for the Word as for the community. In order not to be chained to the text, to be able to enter into a living and sympathetic relationship with the assembly, to be able to underline the heart of the message of each biblical reading, the reader needs to proclaim the text as if one knew it by heart.

Ancient Jewish tradition gives us precious recommendations in this regard. Here is the magnificent example of Rabbi Aqiba (†c.135):

> It happened one day that the leader of the synagogue called upon Rabbi Aqiba to do the public reading of the Torah. But he did not wish to mount [the ambo]. His disciples therefore said to him: "Master, have you not taught us this: that the Torah is life for you, and length of days? Why have you refused to act in consequence?" He replied to them: "By the worship of the Temple! I refused to do the reading solely because I had not read through the text two or three times beforehand. For a person does not have the right to proclaim the words of the Torah before the community if they have not said them to themselves two or three times beforehand. Thus God himself acted. . . ." When he was on the point of giving the Torah to the

[22] OLM, 55, GIRM, 66.
[23] Toukârâm, Psaumes du pèlerin, Éd. Gallimard, Paris, 1956, 136.

Israelites, then, according to Job 28:27, *he saw it, then he evaluated it, then he scrutinized it.* Then it is said that he gave it to humanity.[24]

Such a veneration honors the faithful of the first Covenant. It is eminently fitting for the servants of the new Covenant.

Dignity and beauty

In the tradition of the synagogue, the reading of the sacred text was hardly ever done without chanting. It was taught that the one who reads Scripture without chanting, is guilty of idolatry. Popular language spoke without distinction of singing or of reading a canticle.[25] The Word of God was conceived of as divine music which had erupted on the earth. Clement of Alexandria, (†before 215) wrote with enthusiasm: "The prophets speak, the sound of the music is spread abroad."[26]

A similar chanting of sacred texts is found in numerous religious traditions, most especially in the Islamic tradition that traces chanting of the Koran back to the prophet himself.[27] It may be explained by the desire to tear the sacred word from the banality of a profane reading and to amplify its inherent worth by the magic of melody and rhythm.

We may note that certain languages that are called primitive are often very rich on the level of melody and rhythm, whereas our European languages, which are more intellectual, are poor on the musical level. We may think of the case of African tonal languages: the problem of chanting does not occur for these languages since every word is sung and every song is rhythmed. I keep the memory of these assemblies, chanting the sacred texts according to moving, mysterious melodies, which our Western ears cannot retain, with the great, swaying rhythms of the palm trees which dance in the tornado.

What can we do in our Western languages?

[24] Strack-Billerbeck, *Kommentar zum Neuen Testament aus Talmud und Mishna,* vol. 14, München, 1961, 158.
[25] *Ibid.* 394–398.
[26] *Le Protrepique,* XII, 119. *SC,* 2, 1949, 189.
[27] Cf. Si Boubakeur Hamza, *Le Coran, Traduction nouvelle et commentaires,* coll. "Le trésor spirituel de l'humanité," Fayard, Paris, 1972, 1286–1293.

Renewal unceasingly poses new exigencies. We are placed, affirms John-Paul II, in the face of "a new responsibility towards the Word of God transmitted in the liturgy." The singing and the reading must express "a simplicity, and at the same time, a dignity in which the particular character of the sacred text is resplendantly shown forth, whether in reading or in singing."[28] This is well said. More difficult to realize. We are, without doubt, only at the beginning of research in this area. After having passed from chanting in Latin, which reduced all the texts to a single mode, to an unadorned reading in the vernacular, we must find new formulas to dress the texts in beauty and to make the reading into a real celebration.[29] Scrupulous respect for the literary genre of each text is the least we can demand. The most lyric poetry can be ruined if it is read as if it were prose, and the best story loses its charm if it is presented as if it were poetry. A lamentation does not present itself in the same way as a thanksgiving, the account of a miracle does not resemble a parable. The Word expresses its full efficacy if it keeps the original character that the Spirit of God has given it.

A last remark. Often the texts are read too quickly. The text resounds in the ears but remains on the surface of the heart; the mind does not have the time to make it its own. Always the same formalism is being played out: text proclaimed, rubric done. We stuff people with words but we do not give them the time to "eat" the Word, to taste the honey. When the prophet Ezekiel ate the book of the Word that was given to him, he said: "In my mouth it was as sweet as honey."[30] In order that the wisdom texts distill the savor of a maxim, or that the prophetic oracles may shake the rigidity of our customary ways of acting, or that the theological texts— those of which Paul has the secret and which we must read twice in order to unravel the confusion—may develop the force of their argument, in other words, in order that the Word may open our heart so that the bitter water of our human illusions may flow out from it and that living water, which springs up into life eternal,[31]

---

[28] *Dominicae Coenae* (24 February 1980) 10.

[29] J. Lebron in J. Gelineau, *Dans vos assemblées*, Desclée, 1989, 423–424, suggests punctuating the text with a refrain by the assembly when the text is long. We have published the four Passion accounts, dividing them into ten episodes, each episode concluded by a solo invocation, a choir acclamation, and an invocation by the assembly (North American Liturgy Resources, Phoenix, 1989–1990).

[30] Ezra 3:3.

[31] Cf. John 4:14.

may flow into it, a wise slowness is necessary. The grace of time is required.

We sometimes forget this, as children of a civilization of reading and not of hearing, and we consider that a quick reading is the ideal. We bring our customary attitudes to the ambo. But the Bible was born in a civilization where the Word was queen. We must let the reading do its work in a certain given duration. God cannot be listened to while hurrying.

7
Objects—Places—Rites

The tradition of the Church and the rubrics (which are generally only the transcription in rules or counsels of the givens of the tradition) surround the proclamation of the Word with a certain ceremonial. The elements involved in this ceremonial are diverse. There are objects, like the Lectionary and the Book of the Gospels. There are places, like the *ambo*, the place of the Word, which are linked to the altar, the place of the Eucharist. There are rites, such as the enthronement of the Book of the Gospels on the altar and the procession that bears the Book of the Gospels from the altar to the ambo. There are songs, such as the acclamation of the Gospel.

It is wise to know what the Missal proposes and try to realize this in the best way possible. The best way of honoring the tradition is not necessarily to reactualize it indefinitely, in a repetitive manner, but also to prolong it by new developments.

We should not exaggerate the importance of particular rites nor place them on a pedestal of honor. They are only rites: their value lies in the interior devotion that they create, accompany, or evoke. A celebration of the Word can fully attain its end— the ever deepening entry of the community into the Covenant— without any ritual ceremonial, as without any song and any music. But song, music and rites can allow us to draw near to God. This is what forms the dignity of the rites.[1]

---

[1] We shall not discuss here certain technical aspects of the proclamation of the Word in public. One may find useful aids in C. Duchesneau, *Parole du Seigneur*, Le Centurion, Paris, 1981.

The Book of the Gospels and the Lectionary

The Missal provides for carrying the Book of the Gospels in procession both in the entrance procession at the beginning of the Mass and during the singing of the Alleluia.[2] These rites obviously assume the presence of a book of some beauty, in any case venerable enough to be carried in a procession. One does not carry an ordinary book in a procession, much less a booklet such as a missalette for the faithful.

But on the other hand, a Lectionary is needed on the ambo (lectern) for the two readings that precede the Gospel and eventually for the Responsorial Psalm.

Therefore the ideal would be to use both a Lectionary and a Book of the Gospels (as formerly, when the readings were in Latin). This is what the *Ordo Lectionum* recommends.

> The ancient custom is recommended of having separate books, one for the gospels and the other for the readings for the Old and the New Testament.[3]

The Book of the Gospels

The ritual highlights the proclamation of the Gospel. This solemnization of the Gospel does not mean that the other readings are less important. All of Scripture possesses the same supreme dignity: it is the Word of God, the presence of the Spirit. On the level of revelation, certain of the Old Testament passages are richer than certain pericopes of the Gospels. But the ritual accords a preeminence to the Gospel, in that it reveals more immediately the presence of Christ, the center of Scripture. The *Ordo Lectionum Missae* affirms that "the proclamation of the Gospel constitutes the "high point of the liturgy of the Word."[4]

Tradition, the wisdom of the past, teaches us to surround the book that contains the Word of Jesus with honor. Since the fifth/sixth century some books were written in letters of gold on purple parchment. It is in the Evangeliaries that the art of illuminating reaches the summit of its splendor. The covers are extravagantly

---

[2] *GIRM*, 82c and 94.
[3] *OLM*, 113.
[4] *OLM*, 13.

sumptuous. For example, a golden Evangeliary from the tenth-eleventh century, a gift of Charles V in 1379 and preserved formerly at St. Chapelle, has thirty-five sparkling sapphires, twenty-four rubies, thirty emeralds, and a hundred and four pearls.[5] Tradition complacently justifies such opulence:

> Rupert de Deuts (†1129/1130) notes that it is right that the books of the Gospels are decorated with gold, silver, and precious stones. In them the gold of heavenly wisdom gleams resplendently, the silver of faith's eloquence shines, and the precious stones of the miracles worked by the hands of Christ sparkle.[6]

In a general way the Evangeliary is the richest treasure of the Byzantine churches. Its sumptuousness could be compared to the sumptuousness that the Roman rite used to accord to monstrances.

Today it is not a question of slavishly recopying the richness of the past. Rich is not necessarily synonymous with beauty. One may think that the simplicity of poverty goes well with a book that proclaims: "Happy the poor." Luxury in the Church is often a lack of taste, sometimes a fault. Yet we can allow ourselves to be taught by the spirit and wisdom of tradition. The veneration for the Gospel was expressed formerly through certain artistic forms: today it must seek and find new forms. The *Ordo Lectionum* writes with lyricism:

> The proclamation of the gospel always stands as the high point of the liturgy of the word. Thus the liturgical traditions of both the East and the West have consistently continued to preserve some distinction between the books for the readings. The Book of the Gospels was always designed with the utmost care and was more ornate and shown greater respect than any of the other books of readings. In our times also, then, it is very desirable that cathedrals and at least the larger, more populous parishes and the churches with a larger attendance possess a beautifully designed Book of the Gospels, separate from the other book of readings.[7]

---

[5] In December 1983, a book from the twelfth century, *Les Évangiles d'Henri le Lion*, decorated with illuminations by the monk Herrmann, from the abbey of Helmarshausen between 1173–1175, was sold at auction in London for the sum of 8,140,000 pounds sterling (see *Figaro*, December 7, 1983).

[6] *De divinis officiis*, book 2, c. 23. *PL* 170, 53 D. Concerning Rupert de Deutz, see J. Gribomont in *Rupert de Deuts, Les oeuvres du Saint Esprit*, Coll. "Sources Chrétiennes," 131 (Paris, 1967) 6–17.

[7] *OLM*, 36.

The *Ordo Lectionum* is optimistic when it sees the future filled with liturgical spendors. Certain communities have started on this path of beauty. For example, among German speaking communities, the Benedictine abbey of Sankt Ottilien has edited a Book of the Gospels with twenty-five illuminated pages. B. Kleinheyer affirms: "Those who are for the solemn entrance procession with the Book of the Gospels, for the procession which prepares for the proclamation of the Gospel at the ambo, and who wish to underline that the altar which becomes the table of the Lord is also the table from which one takes the bread of the Word, must be for the publication of a special Book of the Gospels, of a book of solemn character.[8]

What can communities that cannot prepare a special Book of the Gospels do? These communities are far more numerous in the world (in certain African missions, there may be up to ten different language groups).

We presume that the community has a text for the first two readings at the ambo. The book from which the Gospel will be proclaimed can thus be transformed into a Book of the Gospels. A more worthy cover may be given to it than the normal commercial type. It would be surprising to find that there was not an "artist" in the community who could create this work of quality. An icon of Christ or a Cross, or the Greek letters *Alpha* and *Omega* could be placed on the cover. Love for the Word of God will make us inventive.

The Lectionary

The dignity of the Book of the Gospels must draw the Lectionary itself along the same path. With wisdom, the *Ordo Lectionum* notes:

> Along with the ministers, the actions, the lectern, and other elements, the books containing the readings of the word of God remind the hearers of the presence of God speaking to his people. Since, in liturgical celebrations the books too serve as signs and symbols of the sacred, care must be taken to ensure that they truly are worthy and beautiful.[9]

[8] Cited in *Notitiae*, 228–229, 1985, 448.
[9] *OLM*, 35.

If only the entire celebration—not only the proclamation of the Word—could be like the epiphany of God's own beauty in the midst of his people!

THE ENTHRONEMENT OF THE BOOK OF THE GOSPELS ON THE ALTAR

The Rite

The Missal provides for the placement of the Gospel Book on the altar before the proclamation of the Gospel. This placement is practically the equivalent of an "enthronement" (similar to the "exposition" of the Holy Sacrament on the altar). Three possibilities are proposed:

• The Book of the Gospels is placed on the altar before the Eucharistic celebration.[10]

• It is placed on the altar at the beginning of the celebration by the reader or the deacon who has carried it during the entrance procession.[11]

• The reader carries it to the altar after the first readings and before the reading of the Gospel.[12]

The best solution on a liturgical level, and that is directed by the rubrics, is for the community to make use of both a Lectionary and a Book of the Gospels. The Lectionary is placed on the lectern before Mass.[13] The Book of the Gospels is placed on the altar from where it will be taken for the proclamation of the Gospel.

Its significance

What is the significance of this rite? The placement on the altar confers an exceptional honor on the Book of the Gospels. In liturgical tradition the altar is

[10] *GIRM*, (79): (Before the Mass) "the Gospel Book, if distinct from the book of other readings, may be placed on the altar, unless it is carried in the entrance procession."

[11] *GIRM*, 79, 82c, 84, and 129.

[12] *OLM*, 17: "It is most fitting that the deacon, or in his absence the priest, take the Book of the Gospels from the altar" (ex altari). Remember that according to the ancient *Ritus servandus*, V, 5 (before the Council), the deacon placed the Gospel Book on the altar saying the prayer *Munda cor meum*, then took the Gospel Book again from the altar.

[13] *GIRM*, 80.

- the sign of Christ himself, the place at which the mysteries of salvation are exercised, and the center of the assembly, to which the greatest reverence is due.[14]
- the center of the thanksgiving accomplished fully through the Eucharist.[15]

The new ritual for the consecration of churches sums up the teaching of the Christian tradition in this aphorism: *Altare Christus est*, the altar is Christ.[16]

Also, until the ninth and tenth centuries, only the Eucharist and the Book of the Gospels enjoyed the privilege of being placed on the altar. This rule still exists in certain Eastern rites. According to the ancient rituals for the consecration of altars, the bishop places the beginnings of the four Gospels on the altar. We also know that at the time of the celebration of the Councils, the Book of the Gospels was solemnly enthroned on the altar, as though to signify that Christ was presiding in person over the assembly gathered together in his name. Cyril of Alexandria concerning the Third Ecumenical Council at Ephesus in 431 said:

> The holy Synod, assembled at the Church dedicated to Mary, instituted Christ as it were as member and head of the Council. Thus, the venerable Gospel was placed on a throne.[17]

Let us remember that Vatican II took up again with magnificent splendor this rite of enthroning the Book of the Gospels.

The significance of these rites is luminous. When the priest takes the Book of the Gospels from the altar, the sign of Christ, he signifies with splendor that the words he is to proclaim are not his own, but the words of Jesus. The Council says "Christ speaks when the Holy Scriptures are read in the church."[18] It is this affirmation that the rite of the enthronement of the Book of the Gospels underlines with majesty.

---

[14] Instruction *Eucharisticum mysterium*, 24. Doc. caft 69 (1967) col. 1105.
[15] *GIRM*, 259.
[16] *Ordo dedicationis Ecclesiae et altaris* (May 27, 1977 c. 4, 4. You will find in this ritual, c. 4, 1-5, the essential of the symbolism of the altar. Cf. *Notitiae*, 133–135 (1977), pp. 378–380. Remember that in 1 Cor 10:16-20, Paul traces a parallel between communion in the Eucharistic bread which is communion in the body of Christ and communion at a pagan altar, which is communion with the demons.
[17] *Apologeticus ad Theodosium Imp.* PG 76, 472 CD.
[18] *The Constitution on the Sacred Liturgy*, 7.

The altar is also the center of the celebrating assembly. Therefore it is in this center that the Word of Jesus is rooted. It is from this center that it sheds its light over the community. Particularly significant is the enthronement of the Book of the Gospels before the celebration: upon entering the church, the faithful find themselves welcomed in some way by Christ. It is in this spirit that some communities keep the Book of the Gospels enthroned on the altar even outside the times of celebration. It would be a welcome development if this custom would be routine in our Roman rite.

This significance is so much more strongly expressed when, following the ancient tradition, only the Book of the Gospels and the Eucharistic Body of the Lord are placed on the altar. As the Missal says, candles should be placed "around the altar to create a harmonious whole."[19] The Cross should be placed away from the altar: on the altar it is useless; it bears the image of Christ whereas the Eucharistic celebration is going to make the very Body of Christ present.[20]

With even stronger reason, objects that have no purpose in being there, such as the cruets of water and wine, with the bowl for washing hands, and its towel, without forgetting the plastic under the bowl,[21] should be removed. When one is invited to dinner, one does not wash one's hands at the family table. Why then, do some priests wash their hands at "the Lord's table?"[22] In the same way, when one has wiped one's hands, one does not place the towel on the family table. Why then, let the towel lie on Christ's table? It is very simple to carry out these rites in a discrete manner, away from the altar.

Allow me these remarks. I sincerely wish that they were totally

[19] GIRM, 269.
[20] GIRM, 270. To be precise, it must be noted that the Missal allows the placement of candles and a cross on the altar. But the symbolism of the altar, and also, let us say, good liturgical sense, suggests placing them somewhere else in the sanctuary, not on the altar: one does not put candles or a cross on what one venerates as the "sign of Christ"!
[21] These are the words of wisdom that the bishops of the United States proposed when they wrote: "The altar is holy and sacred for the celebrations and the gathering of the community. It must never be used as a clearing table for placing papers, notes, cruets, or anything else." (Bishops' Committee on the Liturgy, *Environment and Art in Catholic Worship*, 71 (Washington 1978, 37).
[22] 1 Cor 10:21.

unnecessary! But when one encumbers the altar with no matter what and litters it with bric-a-brac (book rest, cross holder, candle holder, cruet holder, bowl, towel, sometimes even an eyeglass holder), then one has destroyed the symbolism of the altar.

Allow me a personal memory. I was in Assiout, in Middle Egypt, for a Bible course. The bishop of the Coptic rite invited me one day to visit his cathedral. I accepted very willingly. It was a church of beautiful proportions, without architectural pomposity. When we had entered and were approaching the sanctuary, the bishop said to me thoughtfully: "Of course, you can keep your shoes on for this visit." I had already taken them off discretely, for I knew that Coptic Christians only entered the sanctuary barefoot. We made a tour around the altar, venerating it. A little boy, carrying a cross, preceded us, as if our visit had been a liturgical celebration. Then we went out of the sanctuary walking backwards, for, according to Coptic tradition, the priest, out of respect, always faces the altar, and therefore, never has his back to it.

I do not want to propose that we should "Copticize" our Roman liturgy. It has its particular beauty, woven with sobriety and clarity. But we can allow ourselves to be usefully instructed by the spirit of the Eastern liturgies. In contact with them, we can rekindle the veneration due to the altar, the sign of Christ and the center of the celebrating community. In any case it is clear that the symbolism of the Book of the Gospels on the altar expresses its powerful significance only if the symbolism of the altar itself is first placed in full light.

THE AMBO, PLACE OF THE WORD OF GOD

The biblical ancestor of our present pulpit is the wooden platform that Ezra had built for the solemn reading of the Law[23] at the Feast of Tabernacles in about the year 445 (Neh 8:4).

[23] It is possible that the account of Neh 8 reflects some ulterior uses of the synagogal service. Concerning the pulpit see some indications in *The Jewish People in the First Century*, vol. 2 (Van Gorcum, Assen, Amsterdam, 1976), 940; C. Perrot, *op. cit.*, 134–135.

Yesterday and Today

We could speak today about the "great poverty" of the ambos in certain of our churches. The Council reform has not yet succeeded in persuading all pastors of the necessity of a true ambo. Some icebergs need more to melt them. There are, of course, incontestable successes. But also much indifference. We see everything: shabby reading stands, which were collecting dust in sacristies and which now find themselves totally surprised to be installed in the sanctuary. Lecterns of redundant majesty, behind which the reader disappears, allowing only a head to emerge from between two wings of an eagle. Sometimes only a simple microphone, that is moved from right to left, as in a weekend sports program. One dreams of an ambo which would be majestic while remaining simple, an ambo which would be like a monstrance of the Word of God.

The past invented splendors. Certain pulpits in our cathedrals are true jewels in stone. They were not stingy on dimensions: the pulpit of St. Agnello of the sixth century at Ravenna is six and a half meters long and three meters high.[24] Nor were they sparing on ornamentation: on December 24, 563, at the dedication of St. Sophia at Constantinople (rebuilt after the earthquake of 558), Paul the Silent composed a poem in which he described the ambo:

> This ambo consisted of a great rostrum set up toward the center of the building, under the cupola. Its bulk made it resemble a tower, dazzling with the glistening of innumerable precious stones imbedded in marble of the rarest and most striking shades. The eye rested on surfaces of silver and ivory that added, through contrast, to the sparkling of the gold. Above the rostrum rose a dome covered with gold plate enriched with stones and crowned by a cross.[25]

Even making allowances for poetic lyricism and Mediterranean grandiloquence, we can assume that this pulpit had to look stunning.

Between the ambo-monument of St. Sophia of former times, and the ambo-pulpit of today, there is no doubt a middle course,

---

[24] It can be seen in the principle nave of the basilica of Duomo (founded in the fifth century and reconstructed several times since then).

[25] *Description ambonis.* PG 86, 2251–2264. Text quoted by H. Leclercq, art. "Ambon" in *DACL.* vol. 1 (Letouzey and Ané, 1907), col. 1333. In this article you will find the essential witnesses to the ancient ambons (col. 1330–1347). On Paul the Silent, see O. Bardenhewer, *Les Pères de l'Eglise,* vol. 3 (Bloud and Barrak, Paris, 1899) 14–15.

of architectural moderation and of wise beauty. What does the liturgy judge to be desirable today?

A place for the Word

In the chapter entitled "The Ambo, the place where one proclaims the Word," the Missal proposes that

> the dignity of the Word of God requires the church to have a suitable place for announcing this Word and toward which the attention of the faithful may turn spontaneously during the liturgy of the Word.
>
> As a general rule this place should be a fixed pulpit and not a simple movable stand. The ambo should be arranged according to these requirements, keeping in mind the structure of each church, in such a way that the faithful may see and hear the ministers well.
>
> The readings, the responsorial psalm, and the *Exsultet* are proclaimed from the ambo; the homily and Prayer of the Faithful may also be given from the ambo.
>
> It is hardly suitable for the commentator, the cantor, or the choirmaster to use the ambo.[26]

One can see that these are only very simple directions, easy to carry out, and full of good sense.

They are taken up, amplified, and sometimes clarified in the *Ordo Lectionum:*

> There must be a place in the church that is somewhat elevated, fixed, and of a suitable design and nobility. It should reflect the dignity of God's Word and be a clear reminder to the people that in the Mass the table of God's Word and of Christ's Body is placed before them. The place for the readings must also truly help the people's listening and attention during the liturgy of the Word. Great pains must therefore be taken, in keeping with the design of each church, over the harmonious and close relationship of the ambo with the altar. Either permanently or at least on occasions of greater solemnity, the ambo should be decorated simply and in keeping with its design.
>
> Since the ambo is the place from which the ministers proclaim the Word of God, it must of its nature be reserved for the readings, the Responsorial Psalm, and the Easter proclamation (*Exsultet*). The

[26] *GIRM*, 272.

ambo may rightly be used for the homily and the general intercessions, however, because of their close connection with the entire liturgy of the Word. It is better for the commentator, cantor, or director
of singing, for example, not to use the ambo.

In order that the ambo may properly serve its liturgical purpose,
it is to be rather large, since on occasion several ministers must use
it at the same time. Provisions must also be made for the readers
to have enough light to read the text and, as required, to have sound
equipment enabling the congregation to hear them without difficulty.[27]

We have here the essentials of what we should know about the
ambo and about what we are invited to put into practice according to the possibilities of each community and according to the architecture of each church.

A place . . .

Just as the altar is the place for the Eucharist, the ambo is the
place for the Word.
  • This place must be "elevated, well designed, and suitably
noble."
  • It should be visible. Indeed, it is troublesome in an assembly
to hear a voice without knowing where it is coming from.
  • It should be well lit but not overly bright.
  • The reader should also be visible. If the ambo is too high, one
sees only the reader's head.
  • The ambo should be "fixed." Any simple moveable reading
stand will not do. Even if one interprets this directive in minimal
terms, it means at least this: if in place of a stationary ambo, one
has a portable reading stand, because one cannot do otherwise, the
stand should possess at least a certain dignity.

For the Word

The ambo is the place for the Word, not for words.
  • Only the biblical readings are proclaimed from the ambo. The
exception made for the homily and for the universal prayer is based

---

[27] *OLM*, 32–34.

on their connection with the Word. As for the *Exultet*, it may be considered as the Word which announces the resurrection of the Lord.

• All the biblical readings must be done at the ambo,[28] including the Responsorial Psalm which the psalmist proclaims.

• This rule of reading the biblical readings at the ambo should also be followed in the celebration of the hours, even in a small community.

Where should announcements be made? For it is certainly necessary to announce the next parish fair, the parish school's basketball game, or even next Sunday's special collection. Where should one stand to direct the singing of the assembly? All that can very well take place from an ordinary stand, as long as that stand is not a mini-ambo in competition with the place for the Word.[29]

Ambo and altar

This is the ideal place to express symbolically the theology of the two tables and the relationship that unites the ambo to the altar.

There are diverse solutions. The most simple is to construct the ambo from the same material as the altar. If the altar is in cut stone, let the ambo likewise be in cut stone. If it is out of wood, let the ambo also be out of wood. If it possesses a certain style, let this style be reproduced in the ambo. If it is decorated with a beautiful floral arrangement, let a similar floral arrangement be placed in front of the ambo.

It is often impossible to find a good solution to the problem of the pulpit because the altar is immense and "eats up" all the space in the sanctuary.[30]

---

[28] *OLM*, 16.

[29] The Bishops' Committee on the Liturgy in the United States proposes: "A very simple stand not in competition or in conflict with the pulpit, placed whenever it is needed so that one can see and hear, can be used by the cantor, choirdirector, and the minister who reads the announcement. Its place should allow easy communication with the musicians and the assembly. *Environment and Art in Catholic Worship*, op. cit., n. 75, 38–39.

[30] This signifies the great esteem that one has for the Eucharist and the little consideration that one grants the Word. Inversely, some Protestant churches sometimes present an immense pulpit and an insignificant altar: this also is a symbol.

We must return to reasonable dimensions[31] for constructing altars, that fit harmoniously into the sanctuary and allow for the integration of the ambo there.

We spoke above of the great misery of ambos. We may also speak here in a parallel fashion of the great misery of provisional altars: two wretched trellises at the entrance to the sanctuary, a horizontal plank on top, all covered with a bit of material that even a fife would not want. Thus one ruins the symbolism of the altar. Does one not also risk doing harm to the mysteries—of Word and Eucharist—signified by the ambo and the altar?

Place of the ambo

It is impossible to give precise directives. The place of the ambo depends on the architecture of each church and the make up of the sanctuary. Each case is thus unique.

Let us say it clearly: none of our churches from the Middle Ages to the Council have been built for the liturgy of Vatican II. Therefore, there is no shame in laboring to find a solution. We must simply be inventive.

Before rushing into decisions that, without wanting to imitate St. Sophia of Constantinople, nevertheless want to be definitive, it is wise to arrange for temporary ambos. To try different solutions. To keep the best. Before getting involved with something temporary, it is also wise to decide in advance that it will not be used forever.

Decorations

Like the altar, the ambo must be decorated with taste and sobriety.

It is well understood that its best decoration and its primary beauty is the material from which it is composed as well as the harmony of its proportions. But we can also think about decorating it with an Easter candle (or a similar light) or a floral arrangement.

---

[31] A. Lanotte suggests as dimensions for the altar a cube with a side of .9 meters (*Itinéraire pour l'adaptation des églises à la liturgie actuelle*, Duculot, Gemblout, 1965, 22). J. Aubert proposes 1.3 meters, "sometimes less," in the sense of length (*Des églises pour nos assemblees*, Le Centurion, Paris, 1982, 39).

The microphone

The microphone is not an ornament but a tool, sometimes a necessity. It must never mar the ambo. This happens when it is on a stand and is placed near the reader. It is preferable to incorporate it discretely into the ambo.

A place for the Word and a place for the Eucharist

In the oldest Syrian churches that undoubtedly represent the most ancient models of Christian churches,[32] the space was divided. In the center the ambo was situated with the bishop's throne, where the community gathered to celebrate the Word. In the apse, turned toward the East, was the altar, where the Eucharist was celebrated.

Without wanting to play at archeology or at orientalism, we can very well imagine, where it is possible, especially in small communities, that there still be today two places of celebration. The first would gather the community around the Word; the second would gather it around the altar. This arrangement functions very well, provided the community is not too large and that the church lends itself to it.

In the Book of Revelation, the altar in heaven speaks and celebrates the victory of God.[33] Each altar in our celebrations on earth, simply by its beauty, cries out its joy to God in being the throne of the Lamb. In the Book of Exodus, the mercy seat of the sanctuary is the place where God speaks to Moses.[34] Each ambo must proclaim, simply by its splendor, that it is the place where God continues to speak to his people.

THE GOSPEL PROCESSION

"Behold the procession of the holy gospel advances."
Among the processions that take place in the course of the Mass, the Procession of the Gospel should be the most festive and the most joyous.

[32] See L. Bouyer, *Liturgie*, Paris, Cerf, 1967, 27–35.
[33] Rev 16:7.
[34] Exod 25:22.

For while the Entrance Procession, the Procession of the Gifts and of Communion, all have a practical end (to constitute the assembly, to bring the gifts to the altar, to receive Communion), the Procession of the Gospel has as its first and primary end, the glorification of Christ in his Word, and the acclamation of his presence. This is the culminating point of the celebration of the Word.[35] According to the Ordo of the Gallican liturgy (sixth century), the clergy chant "Gates lift high your heads! Grow higher ancient doors! That the Lord of power, the king of glory, may enter (Ps 24:7)!

The Ordo explains: Behold, the procession of the holy Gospel advances, like the power of Christ triumphing over death, accompanied by the aforementioned song and seven candles (which are the seven gifts of the Holy Spirit, or the lights of the old Law crucified by the mystery of the Cross). The deacon goes up to the ambo as Christ ascends to the throne of the Father's kingdom and from there proclaims the gifts of life, while the clerics acclaim: "Glory to you, O Lord!"[36]

The teaching of tradition

The Solemn Exposition of the Book of the Gospels was often accompanied by the chanting of the Trisagion.[37] In the chapter entitled "The Exposition of the Holy Gospel and the hymn of the Trisagion" from his work *Explanation of the Divine Liturgy*, Nicolas Cabasilas[38] notes, not without a touch of pride for the rites proper to his liturgy:

> The priest, standing in the middle before the altar, raises the Gospel Book and shows it to the people, signifying in this way, the coming of the Savior, when he began to manifest himself to the crowds. For the Gospel represents Christ. . . We praise God himself as Trinity,

[35] J. Brinktrine explains that the readings culminate in that of the Gospel. That is why this reading in ancient times was celebrated with particular solemnity (*Die Heilige Messe*, Schöningh, Paderborn, 1950, 109).

[36] K. Gamber, *Ordo Antiquus Gallicans. Der gallikanische Messritus des 6. Jahrhunderts*, Coll. "Textus Patristici et Liturgici," Pustet, Regensburg, 1965, 18.

[37] Found in the West in the antique *Ordo* Gallican (sixth century). See K. Gamber, *Ordo Antiquus Gallicanus*, op. cit., 18. According to K. Gamber, op. cit. 7–8, it is thanks to Hilary of Poitiers (†376), who was exiled into Asia Minor from 356 to 359, that the Trisagion was introduced from the East into the Gallican liturgy.

[38] *Explanation of the Divine Liturgy*, c. 20. Trans. S. Salaville, SC 2 bis (1967) 147–149. Cabasilas was born around 1322–1323. The date of his death is not known.

such as the manifestation of the Savior has taught us. This hymn which we address to him has been transmitted to us by the angels;[39] and it is also taken from the book of the sacred songs of the prophet. It has been gathered by the Church of Christ, who has dedicated it to the Trinity. For the *Hagios*, repeated three times is the acclamation of the angels;[40] the words *"God strong and immortal* are borrowed from blessed David,[41] when he says: *"My soul thirsts for God, the strong and living God."* To gather and reunite these two acclamations and to add the supplication "Have mercy on us," has been the role of the Church, the assembly of those who know and proclaim the mystery of the Trinity in a single God. . . . This is why we sing this hymn after the showing and the entrance of the Gospel, as though to proclaim that in coming among us, Christ has placed us with the angels and established us in the angelic choirs.

The chant of the Trisagion is found in a number of Eastern liturgies.[42] Nicolas Cabasilas adds the wonderful idea that the coming of Christ in his Word unites the choir of the faithful on earth with the choir of the angels in heaven. This theme is echoed in the Sanctus of the Roman Mass where we likewise acclaim the Lord *una voce*, with one voice. There is, in fact, a parallel between the mystery of the Word and the mystery of the Eucharist: The Church on earth and the Church in heaven acclaim the coming of Christ here in the mystery of the Word and there in the mystery of the Eucharist.

Today

Here is what the Roman liturgy provides today for the deacon:

If incense is used, the deacon assists the priest when he puts incense in the censer during the singing of the *Alleluia* or other chant. Then he bows before the priest and asks for the blessing, saying in a low voice: "Father, give me your blessing." The priest blesses him: "The Lord be in your heart." The deacon answers: "Amen." If the Book of the Gospels is on the altar, he takes it and goes to the lectern; the servers, if there are any, precede, carrying candles and the

---

[39] Nicolas Cabasilas makes allusion to the legend according to which the angels revealed the Trisagion to the Christians of Constantinople.

[40] Allusion to Isa 6:3 and Apoc 4:8.

[41] Allusion to Ps 42:3.

[42] See F. E. Brightman, *Liturgies Eastern and Western*, vol. 1 (Oxford: Clarendon, 1896, 1967) 77, 218, 255, 313-314.

censer when used. At the lectern the deacon greets the people, incenses the book, and proclaims the gospel.[43]

The procession of the Book of the Gospels calls to mind the procession of the Torah in the synagogues at the time of the Feast of the Law (simhat Torah): the scrolls of the Law were carried in procession circling seven times in the synagogue. This procession, rather late in Judaism (cf. *The Encyclopedia of the Jewish Religion* 361), is the normal result of the honor due to the Word of God.

When the Mass is celebrated without a deacon, the ritual is fundamentally the same with necessary adaptations:

> During the singing of the *Alleluia* or other chant, . . . the priest . . . bows before the altar and inaudibly says the prayer, "Almighty God, cleanse my heart."
>
> If the Book of the Gospels is on the altar, he takes it and goes to the lectern, the servers, who may carry the censer and candles, walking ahead of him.[44]

Pastoral suggestions

The heart of the rite, if it is envisioned in its most simple but central significance, is thus: the priest takes the Book of the Gospels, the Word of Christ, from the altar, which represents Christ. He carries it to the ambo, the place for the Word of God, while the Lord is acclaimed.

This procession should be carried out at every Mass. Even if one is celebrating during the week before a small assembly, even if limited space does not allow a solemn procession, one should display the Book of the Gospels. The celebrant takes the book from the altar and shows it to the assembly that acclaims Christ. This holding up of the Book of the Gospels is similar to that of the consecrated host and of the chalice at the consecration. Even in the most humble conditions, the rite will keep its clear meaning.

---

[43] *GIRM*, 131. This procession is actually found in the First Ordo Romanus (around 750). The deacon kisses the feet of the bishop, receives his blessing, kisses the Gospel Book, then, accompanied by the censer-bearer carrying the incense and two sub-deacons and two acolytes carrying candles, goes up to the lectern (*Ordo Romanus*, I, 59. See M. Andrieu, *Les Ordines Romanis du Haut Moyen-Age*, Coll. "Spicilegium Sacrum Lovaniense," Louvain, vol. 2, 1948, 87–89.

[44] *GIRM* 93–94.

It is this heart of the rite that the *Directory of Masses for Children* attempts to highlight when it invites children to participate in the procession of the Book of the Gospels:

> The participation at least of some children in the procession with the Gospel shows forth more clearly the presence of Christ proclaiming the word to his people.[45]

CANDLES AND INCENSE

Commenting on the solemnization of the proclamation of the Gospel, M. Denis-Boulet remarks: "All the liturgies of East and West have a procession which precedes the reading: lights and incense honor the carrying of the Book of the Gospels, as in the Entrance procession they honor the pontiff, and for the same motive: they both represent Jesus Christ."[46]

Candles

Biblical tradition

In the Tent of Meeting, which had formerly been the itinerant sanctuary during the sojourn in the Egyptian desert, a lamp was lit to burn "before Yahweh."[47] A golden candelabra with seven branches,[48] which later became the symbol of Israel, was also located there.

In the Book of Revelation, John has kept the images of the lamp and of the candelabra while changing their symbolism. He sees in his inaugural vision the risen Christ, holding in his right hand "the seven golden candelabra, which are the seven churches" to which he will address his letters. He also sees seven lamps of fire burning before the throne in heaven. These are "the seven Spirits of God."[49]

---

[45] Directory of Masses for Children, November 1973, 33.
[46] In A.-G. Martimort, *The Church at Prayer*, Collegeville, The Liturgical Press.
[47] Exod 27:20-21; cf. Lev 24:2-4.
[48] Exod 25:31-40; cf. 37:17-24.
[49] Rev 1:20. The "seven Spirits" designate either the Holy Spirit in her sevenfold perfection (P. Prigent, *L'Apocalypse de saint Jean*, coll. "Commentaires du Nouveau Testament," XIV, Delachaux et Niestlé, Lausanne-Paris, 1981, 85) or the angels that the tradition called "angels of the Face." E. Lohse, *Die Offenbarung des Johannes*, coll. "Das Neue Testament Deutsch," 11, Vandenhoeck & Rupprecht, Göttingen, 1966, 37-38.

Liturgical tradition

In the ancient liturgy of the *Ordines romani*, the candle constituted an escort of honor. Seven torches accompanied the solemn entrance of the bishop and of the Book of the Gospels.[50] These seven torches formed a crown of honor around the altar,[51] then, reduced to six (for reasons of symmetry), they were placed on the altar. The two candlesticks which remain to the two acolytes of the Roman rite represent an organic witness to the ancient splendor of this procession of the Book of the Gospels.

The candle is also a symbol of God. This symbol culminates in the New Testament in the affirmation of Jesus: "I am the Light of the world."[52] During the feast of Tabernacles, where four enormous candlesticks were installed in the temple of Jerusalem, in the court of the women, their light was such, it is said, that it illumined all the interior courts of the holy City.[53] It is in this context that Jesus affirms that he is not only the light of his people, but the light of the whole world.[54]

In the procession of the Book of the Gospels, the symbolism of the lit candle is multiple.

• The light honors the dignity of the Book of the Gospels and, through it, venerates Christ.

• It symbolizes Christ himself whom the Gospel proclaims as the "Light of the World."

• It signifies hope of the eternal day when the whole Church will be transfigured by the light of the Lamb.[55]

In looking at the candle and hearing the words of Christ, Christians pray that their own lives may become Good News and each of them, like Christ and with him, "light of the world."[56]

[50] These seven torches already existed in the ancient Gallican *Ordo*. See K. Gamber, *op. cit.*, 18.
[51] *Ordo Romanus* I, 52. See M. Andrieu, vol. 2, *op. cit.*, 84.
[52] John 8:12.
[53] Cf. Sukkah, 5:2-3. Cf. H. Danby, *The Midrash*, Clarendon Press, Oxford, 1933, 179-180. G. F. Moore, *Judaism in the First Centuries of the Christian Era*, vol. 2, Harvard University Press, Cambridge, 1970, 49-50.
[54] See R. Schnackenburg, *Das Johannes-Evangelium*, II, coll. "Herders Theologischer Kommentar zum Neuen Testament," 1971, 237.
[55] Rev 22:23.
[56] Matt 5:14.

Incense

Biblical tradition

After the example of ancient oriental religions, Israel used incense widely in its worship. In the Temple of Solomon, the altar of incense stood before the Holy of Holies. In the morning and the evening incense was burned there as a symbol of the prayer that rose towards the throne of God in sacrifice of praise.[57]

This golden altar was transported into heaven for the heavenly liturgy according to the Apocalypse. An angel responsible for the service of the altar of incense in heaven could offer both incense and the prayers of the saints on the golden altar placed before the heavenly throne. The twenty-four elders—no doubt the just of the Old Testament[58]—accompanied themselves on harps as they sang the new song and offered golden cups filled with incense, which are the prayers of the saints.[59]

Liturgical tradition

With a past so rich on a biblical plane, incense should have found an easy entry into Christian worship. But in that the pagan cults widely used incense evoked disagreeable memories in the Christian conscience. Justin († c. 165) claimed to know that the demons regaled themselves with incense and profited from it at the expense of those who offered it to them.[60]

In the East the first witness seems to go back to the fourth century. Incense is used during the proclamation of the Gospel. In describing the liturgy of the Sunday vigil in the Church of the Resurrection in Jerusalem, the pilgrim Egeria recounts:

> They brought censers to the interior of the cave of the Anastasis, so that all the basilica was filled with perfume. Then, while the

[57] Cf. Exod 30:1-8; 1 Kgs 6:20-21. Incense was also added to the offerings of wheat flour (Lev 2:1-15) "as a calming perfume" (Lev 2:2-9) and to the show bread (Lev 24:7).
[58] See A. Feuillet, "Les vingt-quatre vieillards de l'Apocalypse," in *RB*, 65, 1958, 5-32.
[59] Rev 5:8 and 8:3-4.
[60] *Second Apology*, 6. The uselessness of the offering of incense is underlined by Athenagorus, *Supplication for the Christians*, 13 (cf. *SC*, 3, 1943, 99), which dates from the year 177, and by Irenaeus, *Against the Heresies*.

bishop stood inside the grilles, he took the Gospel, came to the entrance and read the account of the Lord's Resurrection himself.[61]

In the West it was not until the *Ordines romani* of the seventh and eighth centuries that incense was mentioned. It was carried before the pope and during the procession of the Book of the Gospels.[62] In carrying incense before the Book of the Gospels,[63] the community signified that it was preparing a path of perfume for the Word of Jesus. The incensing of the book itself signified the veneration and prayer that it offered the Gospel. Just as the magi, when they found the Infant King, prostrated themselves before him in a gesture of adoration, and offered him gold, incense, and myrrh,[64] so the Christian community which has found the Messiah-Savior in the Gospel, offers him the incense of its prayer and adoration.

Pastoral suggestions

Candles

The symbolism of light is easy to perceive. The procession with candles is easy to realize. Each time that this is possible, it should be highlighted. It enriches the proclamation of the Gospel with a joyous and festive note. Jerome (†419–420) witnesses for his era: "In all the churches of the East, when the Gospel is to be read, lamps are lit, even if the sun is already shining. This is not to chase away

[61] Egeria's *Diary*.
[62] *Ordo Romanus*, I, 41, 46, 59. Cf. M. Andrieu, vol. 2, *op. cit.*, 80, 82, 87–88.
[63] The Middle Ages, in search of symbolism, sometimes exaggerated the symbolic meaning of rites. On the subject of incense, Durand de Mende (about 1230–1296) explains: "The censer clearly represents the human heart, which must be open on top to receive, and closed at the bottom to keep and retain; it must contain the fire of charity and the incense of devotion, or of a very sweet prayer, or of good examples which tend towards heaven, which are represented by the perfumed smoke which rises from the censer. Just as the incense exhales a sweet perfume into the fire of the censer and rises on high, so the good work or prayer which precedes from charity is more effective than all other perfumes. The censer full of incense represents the body of Christ full of sweetness; the charcoal represents the Holy Spirit; the incense, the savor of good works" *Rational ou Manuel des Divins Offices*, trad. C. Barthelemy, vol. 2, Vivès, Paris, 1854, 44–45. On Durand de Mende, see M. Noirot, in *Catholicisme*, vol. 3, Letouzey et Ané, 1952, col. 1191–1192.
[64] Matt 2:11 reflects back to Isa 60:6 and Ps 72:10-11, 15. See R. Laurentin, *Les Évangiles de l'Enfance du Christ*, Desclée de Brouwer, 1982, 306.

the darkness, but to show forth a sign of joy."[65] This sign of joy is always suitable for our time.

The paschal candle, placed near the ambo, reminds the community that the proclamation of the Gospel is carried out in the light of the resurrection. Only the Risen One can open our hearts to the understanding of the Word.

Incense

The offering of incense is held in high esteem in the Eastern liturgies as in the countries of the Far East.

In contrast, the significance of incense in our European and North American civilizations is less well understood. If such is the case in a community, there is no point in forcing its use. Nor is there much point in engaging in a weighty explanation of its significance. For if there is not agreement between the community and the symbols it uses, it is easy to fall into the trap of ritualism. A symbol is all the more powerful when it does not need to be explained but is understood.

It is useful to add that if one uses incense, it must be used generously. Let the censer smoke happily, let the fire be generous, that the incense may perfume the whole assembly and rise to the rafters! A tiny grain placed on a languishing charcoal will not do. If the rite is bloodless, it no longer has power to speak.

Flowers

Flowers may be used in the Book of the Gospels procession and with the candles form a pleasing environment. One adorns the procession and the ambo with flowers as one adorns the family table with flowers for a festive meal. This use of flowers reminds us of an ancient custom of the Roman Church at the beginning of the third century. Hippolytus of Rome teaches us that they offered and blessed roses and lilies and he adds: "In everything one harvests one gives thanks to the holy God and one uses it for his glory."[66]

[65] *Contra Vigilantium*, 7. PL 23:346.
[66] *Apostolic Tradition*, 32. Cf. L. Deiss, *Springtime of the Liturgy*, Collegeville, The Liturgical Press, 1979.

Dances

Certain communities have integrated liturgical dances in their celebration as an accompaniment for the showing forth and the procession of the Book of the Gospels. Prepared with great care and realized with dignity, these liturgical dances can express the veneration not only of young people but of the whole community towards the Word of God.[67]

This form of art, should "edify"—in the strongest sense of the word—the piety of the community. It can only attain this if it is executed with the perfection that is fitting for beauty offered to God and with the prudence that is fitting when something new is introduced to the celebrating community. This requires simple good sense.

In dancing thus for the Lord, communities accomplish the will of God spoken to us by his Spirit:

Praise God by the dance! (Ps 150:4)

THE ALLELUIA, PROCESSIONAL ACCLAMATION OF THE BOOK OF THE GOSPELS

To accompany the procession of the Book of the Gospels, the liturgy proposes the Alleluia chant (or another acclamation during Lent) and verses which are taken from the Gospel.

Alleluia is the Latin of the Hebrew *Halelu-Yah* which signifies *Praise Yah(weh)*. This invitation to praise is found in those psalms called Alleluia psalms[68] of which certain are part of the Hallel (Ps 113–118) that Christ recited at the Last Supper.[69] The Alleluia does not therefore have to beg the right to be included in the Mass liturgy: it has been at home there since the first Eucharist, and it was the Lord himself who introduced it.

By its joyful and triumphant character, the Alleluia evokes the song of the redeemed Church. In his Nineveh of sadness to which

---

[67] Three choreographies of G. Weyman for the Procession of the Gospel are to be found in L. Deiss, G. Weyman, *Liturgical Dance*. NALR, Phoenix, 1983, 57–73.

[68] Pss 105–107, 111–114, 116–118, 135–136, 146–150.

[69] *Hymnèsantes*, literally, after having sung the hymns, Matt 26:30 and Mark 14:26.

he had been deported, Tobit the Elder did not stop dreaming of a Jerusalem where the houses themselves would sing Alleluia:

The gates of Jerusalem shall resound
with canticles of happiness,
and all its houses will say:
Alleluia! Blessed be the God of Israel! (Tobit 13:17).

In the New Testament the Alleluia is found at the end of the Apocalypse in the triumphant song of the redeemed of the earth. The Alleluia is like a refrain which rhythms their acclamation:

I heard a sound like the voice of an immense crowd in heaven which cried out:
Alleluia!
Salvation, glory and power to our God!
Yes, just and true are his judgments.
Alleluia! . . .
The twenty-four elders and the four living creatures prostrated themselves and adored God who sits on the throne. They said:
Amen! Alleluia!
And I heard a sound like the voice of an immense crowd, like the voice of great waters, like the voice of mighty thunders. They said:
Alleluia! For he reigns,
the Lord our God, the Almighty.
Let us rejoice, let us exult, let us give him glory,
for behold the wedding of the Lamb has come (Rev 19:1-4, 6).

It is thus from the heavenly liturgy that Alleluia is linked to the acclamation of the Gospel. It remains for music to create an environment of splendor. Procession, candles, incense, flowers, dances: all this is useless if the music is not joyful and festive. In the verses, one should avoid falling again into the psalmic genre and swallowing the syllables in the greyness of an overdominant melody.

Plainchant gives us a lesson in beauty. We know that in its golden age it provided exceptional melodies to decorate the *jubilus* of the Alleluias (*jubilus* is the melody that decorates the syllable *Ia* of *Allelu-Ia*). Certain melodies, especially those of the Easter season that sing of the risen Christ, are pure marvels. The murmuring of vocalizations which spring up without end in order to magnify the divine name of Yahweh belong to the greatest of vocal art that the human genius has created. It will take much time, patience, and genius to create the equivalent in the vernacular.

For the musician who judges the order of the notes, the *jubilus* does not have any spiritual significance. The musician admires it as one would delight in the song of the nightingale or the color of the rose. But ancient Christianity discovered in the *jubilus* a particular meaning. Augustine explains:

> Those who sing, whether at the harvest, or the fruit gathering, or in whatever other exalting occupation begin to express their joy in the words of a song. But when they are filled with a joy so great that they can no longer express it in words, they discard the words and begin to *jubilate*. When one sings the *jubilus*, it is as if the heart is involved in that which it cannot express. And to what is this jubilation due, if not to the indescribable God? Indescribable is that which cannot be expressed. If therefore you cannot express it, and on the other hand, you must not keep silence, what remains for you to do but to *jubilate?* The heart rejoices without words and the immensity of its joy is not limited by words.[70]

The song without words can be more significant than the word itself. Certain notes can appear useless in a text but be necessary to the celebration. The *jubilus* is to music what the smile is to joy and what tears are to sadness. It is "a joy without words," as Augustine says,[71] because of the excess of joy.

In the celebration of the Word, we need not only biblical texts clearly proclaimed, and homilies intelligently structured, well-adapted universal prayers—all elements which satisfy the understanding. We also need beauty to make the heart sing.

Psalm 150, which serves as a final doxology to the whole psalter, invites the universe of heaven and earth to praise God to the sound of all the musical instruments. The invitation *Halelu* returns ten times. These ten Halelu seem to echo the "words of the Covenant, the ten words"[72] that God gave as the Law to the Hebrew people on Sinai[73] according to the tradition. In Jesus, the ancient Law has become the Gospel. The Alleluia of the Gospel acclaims the One who is the Word of the new Covenant, Jesus Christ.

---

[70] *Enarratio in Ps 32:8. PL* 36:283.
[71] *Enarratio in Ps 99:4. PL* 37:1212.
[72] Exod 34:28.
[73] A. Ariens, *Die Psalmen im Gottesdienst des Alten Bundes*, Paulinus-Verlag, Trier, 1961, 177.

THE KISSING OF THE BOOK OF THE GOSPELS

After the proclamation of the Gospel, the priest kisses the Book of the Gospels.[74] This custom continues the tradition of the synagogue which kissed the scroll of the Torah after the reading.[75] In certain communities until the thirteenth century, all the clergy kissed the Book of the Gospels.[76] In the Coptic liturgy still today, the people are familiar with this gesture of the clergy.[77]

Kissing the Book of the Gospels is a gesture of tenderness and of veneration in regard to the Word of Christ. In ancient times one placed one's hand to the mouth (*ad-os, adoration*) to send a kiss to someone (this was the way of venerating the idols), or one brought the edge of one's garment to the mouth, a gesture that is still used in the East.

This kiss is accompanied by a petition for forgiveness. At the same time as he kisses the Book of the Gospels, the priest says: "May the Gospel wipe away our sins."

[74] GIRM, 95.

[75] R. Tournay, in *Assemblées du Seigneur*, 88, 1966, 60.

[76] J.-A. Jungmann, *Missarum Solemnia*, vol. II, Aubier, 1952, 220.

[77] R. Cabié, *The Church at Prayer*, vol. 2, *The Eucharist*. Collegeville: The Liturgical Press, 1986.

Conclusions:
Balance Sheet and Prospects

BALANCE SHEET
WORD OF GOD AND THE COVENANT

We have affirmed the extreme importance (*maximum momentum*) of the Word of God. The Word of God creates the universe, and especially that universe of love that is the ecclesial community.

The importance of the Word of God is the same as that of the Eucharist. There is a real presence of Christ in the Word as in the Eucharist, even if this presence is not sacramental. This is why the veneration due the Word is the same as that due the Eucharist.

The Eucharist is the celebration of the new Covenant. "This is the blood of the new Covenant," says Jesus at the Last Supper, taking up the words of Moses on Sinai. The first Covenant is founded on the Word proclaimed by Moses and accepted by the community. The new Covenant, like the first, is founded on the Word proclaimed at Mass and accepted by the community. This is why the liturgy of the Word and the liturgy of the Eucharist are so intimately linked that they form but a single act of worship. And this single act of worship is the celebration of the new Covenant.

On a pastoral level there must never be a celebration of the Eucharist without a real celebration of the Word. Nor must there be a celebration of the Word without the grace of the Eucharist, in other words, without spiritual communion.

THE RESPONSORIAL PSALM

The Responsorial Psalm responds to the Word which has been proclaimed. True "canticle of the Covenant," it does not have a particular literary genre, but adopts that of the psalm from which it is taken.

There is a story of Jesus in the psalms. They reveal Christ, they are epiphanies of his face. One cannot replace the Responsorial Psalm by an ordinary chant, however beautiful it may be, just as one cannot replace the Gospel by an ordinary reading, however religious it may be, or the face of Jesus by the face of an ordinary man, however great a poet he may be.

THE HOMILY

In its simplest form, the homily is the translation of the Word of God. The most significant example is the homily of Ezra: Ezra reads the biblical text in Hebrew; the text is translated into the common language of the people. In its highest form, the homily is the actualization of the Word for the celebrating community. The most significant example is the homily of Jesus at Nazareth: "Today this Word which you have just heard is accomplished."

To attain its end, the homily must pass by the path of literal sense (what does this word mean in its literal sense?), by the path of Christological sense (how is Christ presented in this text?), and by the path of actualization (what does this text mean today for the community?

The homily is the Word of God at the level of the celebrating community.

The ministry of the Word is entrusted to all the baptized. This ministry is exercised under the responsibility of the one who presides in the community.

Prayer to the Spirit of Jesus is the ordinary path to understanding the words inspired by the Spirit. The homily itself may become prayer.

THE UNIVERSAL PRAYER OR
PRAYER OF THE FAITHFUL

"In the universal prayer or prayer of the faithful, the people exercise their priestly function and intercede for all of humanity" (GIRM, 45)."

This prayer is rooted in the Word of God which in a certain sense is sown in the community. It opens itself to the dimension of humanity, it represents the part that each community, including the smallest, takes in the suffering and joy of all people.

THE ACTORS OR CELEBRANTS

It is the entire assembly which celebrates the Word. Each member of the faithful is a "celebrant" according to the ministry entrusted to them and the place they occupy.

It belongs to the presider to assume responsibility for all that is done under his authority. It belongs to the reader and to the psalmist not first of all to read or to sing the Word, but, in reading or singing, to make it understood by the community.

OBJECTS, PLACES, RITES

The tradition of the Church and the rubrics of the Missal surround the proclamation of the Word with ceremony. It is good to be familiar with and to celebrate them according to the traditions of the community.

It is desirable to have a Lectionary and especially a Book of the Gospels that is worthy of the Word.

The Book of the Gospels should be placed on the altar before the reading of the Gospel. This is an "enthroning" of the Book of the Gospels.

The ambo is the place of the Word of God. Its style and its decoration should direct one back to the altar. Thus a theology of the two tables is put into relief: that of the Word and that of the Eucharist.

The ritual calls for the Procession of the Gospel: the Book of the Gospels is taken from the altar, the sign of Christ, and carried to the ambo, the place of the Word. This procession may be solemnized by candles and incense. Certain communities add flowers and dance.

The Alleluia (or the acclamation which replaces it) is the song that accompanies this procession.

Many parish communities give fitting splendor to the celebration of the Word. Others need to improve in this regard.

PROSPECTS

Vatican II highlighted "the central character of the Word of God in the life of the Church."[1] The Council underlines this central character in placing the Word on the same level as the Eucharist: "The Church has always venerated the divine Scriptures just as it has always venerated the Body of Christ."[2]

This rediscovery of the Word is today for the Church the most fantastic opportunity that has been given to it in centuries. This opportunity has not come to it by chance. It is the fruit of the biblical and the liturgical movements that have marked Catholicism during the last century. Vatican II was the meeting place of these two movements.

The biblical movement grew dramatically in the nineteenth century by the extraordinary discoveries in the Fertile Cresent (the first extra-biblical account of the Deluge, discovered at the site of Nineveh, was only decoded in 1872 by G. Smith). These discoveries totally renewed the biblical landscape which, for two thousand years were fixed in the immobility of antique ruins. The interpretations held as traditional since time immemorial—such as the historicity of the Deluge or the Tower of Babel—dissolved into dust as the texts revealed their authentic religious message. In the Catholic community, the movement found a promotor of exemplary courage in Father Lagrange, founder of the École Biblique in Jerusalem.[3] The terrible tempests of the modernist crisis (the decree *Lamentabili* of Pius X dates from 1907), far from halting the advance of the biblical movement, forced it to exercise greater prudence and diligence in its scientific exploration. The movement finally obtained its liberty in *Divino Afflante* of 1943. Vatican II, in the Constitution on Revelation (*Dei Verbum*) accorded it its benediction in 1965.

---

[1] E. Bianchi, in *La réception de Vatican II*, coll. "Cognitatio fidei," 134, 1985, 157.
[2] *Dei Verbum*, 21.
[3] See R. De Vaux, "Le Père Lagrange," in *Bible et Orient*, coll. "Cognitatio fidei," 24, 1967, 9–22.

The liturgical movement was undertaken and maintained in the last century by Benedictine abbeys: in France by the abbey of Solesmes (opened by Dom Guéranger in 1833), in Belgium by the abbeys of Maredsous and Mont César, and in Germany by Maria Laach. It received a precious encouragement from Pius X in the *Motu proprio* on sacred music, in 1903, and in the decree *Sacra Tridentina* on frequent Communion in 1905. At the time of the Second World War, it spread from the high places of the Benedictine tradition into the plains of Christianity, beginning in the most open and the most missionary parishes. The encyclical *Mediator Dei* of Pius XII that blessed the movement (with certain cautions about usage) dates from 1947, the restoration of Holy Week from 1955, and the Constitution of the Liturgy of Vatican II from 1963.

The celebration of the Word benefits from the vitality of these two movements. It is the biblical movement entering into each church, into each community, into each celebration. It is the liturgical movement joining itself to the biblical movement and inheriting its riches.

No one would dare to affirm that before Vatican II the Church did not know or celebrate the Word nor organize authentic liturgies. But Vatican II has been like a spring which, after centuries of winter, has permitted the biblical and liturgical sap to burst forth into a thousand blossoms.

What is the future of this spring? No one can predict it. No one knows where we are going, where the Spirit of Jesus will guide us. Between spring and the beginning of summer there is often a period in which the last nocturnal frosts can still attack the fruit trees in flower and destroy all hope of fruit. We have already known these periods since Vatican II (ultraconservative or progressive frost). We shall know others in the future. Our hope remains. The permanent reform (*perennis reformatio*) of which the Council spoke is in process, however slow the spring.[4]

A BIBLICAL CHURCH

The Church does not exist for itself. It only exists to communicate to people eternal life, an eternity of joy, of peace, and of love.

---

[4] Decree on Ecumenism, *Unitatis redintegratio*, 6.

Just as Christ came to the earth "for us humans, and for our salvation," as we say in the Creed, so the Church is only established on earth for us human beings, and for our salvation. Vatican II affirms: "The Church tends towards a single end: that the reign of God may come and that the salvation of human beings may be accomplished. The Church is the sacrament of universal salvation, manifesting and actualizing at one and the same time the mystery of God's love for humankind."[5]

In order to reveal this sign of love and to actualize it effectively in regard to all people, the Church must conform itself to the ideal that God has traced for it. It must be the Church according to the heart of God, the Church such as the Word reveals and fashions. Does it appear as such? Is it effectively such?

The Church of Jesus Christ is a "dwelling place of God among humanity," a Church where the Lord of glory lives in our midst, his sisters and brothers, as in his own house ("We are his house!"), and who wishes that we walk with him, reaching out a hand to the smallest of our sisters and brothers![6] Does the Church appear as the holy dwelling of God among humanbeings? Is it effectively this?

The Church of Jesus Christ is a community of love having but a single heart and a single soul.[7] Does it appear truly as a communion of love in the tenderness of a single heart, in the unity of a single soul? Is the Church effectively this?

The Church of Jesus Christ has as a rule of life to walk "according to the truth in charity."[8] It is a Church whose supreme law is to love God in loving all people, including enemies. Does the Church appear as the mirror of truth, as the home of charity? Is it effectively such?

The Church of Jesus Christ is a family of brothers and sisters, where no one seeks to dominate the other, where "each, by humility, esteems the others as superior to themselves,"[9] where there is only one Father, the heavenly Father, where there is only one Sav-

---

[5] Pastoral Constitution on the Church in the Modern World, *Gaudium et spes*, 45, 1. The expression "sacrament of universal salvation" is a citation of *Lumen Gentium*, 48.

[6] Rev 21:3; Heb 2:11 and 3:6; Matt 25:41.

[7] Acts 4:32.

[8] Eph 4:15.

[9] Phil 2:3.

ior, Christ Jesus.[10] Does the Church appear as a family of sisters and brothers? Is it effectively such?

In this Church-family there is no longer "slave nor free, man nor woman," for all form one in Christ.[11] Does the Church appear as a community that has gone beyond all sexual discrimination? Has it really?

As a Church of the beatitudes, the Church places its happiness in poverty, for Jesus has said: "Blessed are you poor!" It refuses riches because Jesus has said: "Woe to you rich!"[12] Does the Church appear happy to be poor? Is it truly?

It is a holy Church but is composed of sinful members. It is a holy Church in the measure that it recognizes itself as sinner. It is a Church saved in the measure in which it knows itself to be lost, for "the Son of Man has come to seek and save what is lost.[13] It is the Church that St. Ambrose calls, with a malicious smile I imagine, *casta meretrix*, chaste prostitute.[14] The Church prostitutes itself each time it allies itself with money, power, and the pride of this world. It becomes chaste, even more, it becomes *parthenon agnes*, "chaste virgin," as Paul says,[15] by the kiss of Christ. Only a Church which recognizes itself as a sinner can be thus redeemed by Christ. Does the Church effectively recognize itself as a sinner?

It is a Church in which no one dares teach his brother or sister for of the Church of the new Covenant it is said: "They shall all be taught by God," words from the Book of Isaiah which Jesus loved so much that he cited it in the discourse on the bread of life at Capernaum.[16] It is a Church where each must say to their brother and sister: "Let yourself be taught by God." Does the Church really appear as the Church of the new Covenant? It is truly such?

The Gospel is the mirror in front of which the Church must place itself to look at its face. At each celebration, the liturgy of the Word holds out this mirror and asks if it is the "sacrament"—at one and the same time the sign and the reality—of the love of God for the

---

[10] Matt 23:8-9.
[11] Gal 3:28.
[12] Luke 6:20, 24
[13] Luke 19:10.
[14] *Traité sur l'Évangile de saint Luc*, III:23. Cf. *SC*, 45, 1956, 132.
[15] 2 Cor 11:2.
[16] John 6:45, citing Isa 54:13.

world. Does the Church appear today as such in the eyes of the world? Is it effectively so?

The Church has never ceased to keep alive its relation with the Word. It has always been a biblical Church: this is its grace. It has not always been it sufficiently: this is its fault. It must become a biblical Church more and more each day: this is its duty. Each celebration of the Word provides a new opportunity to become a biblical Church.

WORD AND COMMUNITY

With the Corinthians, who are often difficult and sometimes quarrelsome, Paul asks with humor if they have need as do some "super-apostles" who traffic[17] in the Word of God for a letter of recommendation in order to announce to them the Gospel of Jesus Christ. He adds this superb affirmation:

> Our letter is yourselves, a letter written in our hearts, known and read by all. Clearly, you are a letter of Christ written with our help, not with ink, but with the Spirit of God, not engraved on tablets of stone, but in hearts of flesh" (2 Cor 3:2-3).

There is therefore, in the thought of Paul, an identification between the message which he announces to them and the community which receives it. Bearer of the Word, the community becomes in its own turn Word of God for the world. Living according to the Gospel, it becomes itself the Gospel. We can summarize the mystery of the Word and of the community as follows: the Gospel is the book of Christians and the life of Christians is the book for the pagans. Or: the best celebration of the Word is the life of the Christian community.

The mystery of the Word joins that of the Eucharist. The Eucharist makes the Church, the Church makes the Eucharist.[18] One can also affirm that the Word makes the Church. It is the Word of salvation that gives birth and growth to the community of Christians.[19] Inversely, the community of Christians gives birth to the Word. It incarnates each community as an epiphany of the Gospel.

[17] 2 Cor 12:11, 2:17.
[18] H. De Lubac, *Méditations sur l'Église*, Aubier, Paris, 1953, 115, 117.
[19] *Presbyterorum ordinis*, 4.

It would be naive to dream that it suffices to celebrate the Word in order to transform the Church into Word of God and to change each community into a living Gospel. But it would be even more naive to dream that this change may be realized without a constant and faithful celebration of the Word. The more the Word is known, loved, celebrated, the more the community can live according to the Word.

A LOOK AT THE LECTIONARY

The Lectionary is the most extraordinary opportunity of renewal that has been offered to the Church for centuries. But no one is naive enough to think that it is perfect. Here are two reflections about it.

The first concerns the Responsorial Psalm. We may hope for an edition for the Christian community of a psalter containing all the Responsorial Psalms (like the book which gathers together the texts of all the canticles) and gives these psalms in their entirety whenever this seems desirable. Communities would then have a larger access to the psalter. They would not be reduced to listening to the three stanzas given in the Lectionary. They could also by themselves or in dialogue with the psalmist sing and pray the psalms. H. Kraus thinks that the psalter was "the book of song and of prayer of the post-exilic community."[20] It must become once again the book of song and of prayer of the community of the Risen One.

The second remark concerns the Lectionary itself. We have pointed out the difficulty, even the impossibility, of making contact in a sustained manner with an entire biblical book. The present Lectionary spreads out the biblical books either over three years in the Sunday and feastday cycle or over two years in the weekday cycle. In addition, the latter cycle often lacks fundamental biblical passages that are in the former.

For the faithful who participate solely in Sunday or feastday celebrations, or simply from time to time during the week, this is no major inconvenience. The Lectionary opens to them the door to the garden of the Scriptures. It is of little importance by which

[20] *Psalmen,* vol. I, *op. cit.,* 18.

paths the faithful come to the Scriptures or of little importance by which door they enter. The essential is to enter and to meet the God of all marvels there in the beauty of the flowers and the sweetness of the fruits.

But for the faithful who participate in the celebration of daily Mass, one may ask if a second Lectionary, whose use would be optional, would not be a good idea. This weekday Lectionary would follow the biblical books more closely and would give them in a more sustained manner.[21] It would also present shorter pericopes that would allow people to deepen the biblical text. Perhaps in the weekday Masses a single reading with the Responsorial Psalm, followed by a solid homily and a substantial universal prayer, would be more profitable to the community than two readings, sometimes long, which glide over the assembly without satisfying it, as abundant waters run over prairies without penetrating the soil.

These considerations do not cast any shadow on the present Lectionary. They simply remind us that what is desirable is not first of all the good of the Lectionary but the good of the community. The Lectionary is made for the community, not the community for the Lectionary. And the Church is the mistress of the Lectionary.

SUNDAY CELEBRATIONS IN THE ABSENCE OF A PRIEST

The "Sunday celebrations in the absence of a priest" have multiplied in countries long Christian to such a point that an official Directory has been published about them.[22] In fact, these celebrations are not a new phenomena: in mission countries they have been the daily bread for centuries. Some think that they are "an opportunity for the Church."[23] Others suggest "advancing with prudence

---

[21] For example, this ferial Lectionary allows us to celebrate better the Book of Isaiah (the present ferial Lectionary only retains sixteen pericopes of Isaiah 1–39, eleven pericopes of Isaiah 40–55, and four pericopes of Trito-Isaiah 56–66). One would not omit from the Gospel According to Matthew the ministry of John the Baptist (3:1-12), the baptism (3:13-17) and temptation of Jesus (4:1-11), his transfiguration (17:1-9), which would destroy the very structure of the first of the Gospel accounts.

[22] Congregation of Divine Worship, *Directory for Sunday Celebrations in the Absence of a Priest*, 2 June 1988. See *Celebrations in the Absence of a Priest*, Phoenix, NALR, 1989.

[23] R. Coffey, "Église-Assemblée-Dimanche," in *Construire l'Église ensemble*, Éd. du Centurion, Paris, 1976, 126.

but without multiplying this type of gathering, as if it were the best solution and the last opportunity."[24] Let us understand: these celebrations are an opportunity when there is no other celebration possible. But are they an opportunity in comparison with the Mass of which Vatican II affirms: "No celebration can construct itself without finding its root and center in the celebration of the Eucharist."[25]

At the heart of these celebrations is the celebration of the Word of God. The judgment to be made vis-à-vis these celebrations is therefore the judgment one makes on the Word. In other words, if the Word is as venerable as the Eucharist, these celebrations of the Word are as venerable as the celebrations of the Eucharist. If there is a real presence of Christ in the Eucharist, there is also a parallel real presence of Christ in the Word, even if it is not of a sacramental nature. If the Eucharist is the celebration of the new Covenant, the Word, too, allows the community to enter into the new Covenant. The communities which celebrate in the absence of a priest are not orphans: his grace is as powerful in these communities as in those which celebrate the Eucharist.

To affirm these theological realities is not to deprecate the Eucharist; it is simply to realize that the celebration of the Word has its only true value. Let us note that these theological realities are important for the celebrations of the Word among our Protestant sisters and brothers.

These remarks should lessen the lack of ease, sometimes the anguish, of communities without priests. Without doubt this anguish is limited in countries long Christian, for they are never deprived for long periods of ordained ministry. But the situation is totally different for Christians in mission countries, dispersed among animists or Muslims, who only have the joy of celebrating the Eucharist once or twice a year. How, on the other hand, can we bring them Communion[26] from the central mission when the distances are often enormous and the roads in the rainy season impassable? A Christian community without the Eucharist is in an abnormal situation since the Eucharist, according to Vatican II, is "the source and summit of all Christian life."[27] To recognize the value of celebra-

---

[24] Paul VI, Discourse of 26 March 1977, cited in note 20 of *Directoire*.
[25] *Presbyterorum ordinis*, 6, cited in *Directoire*, 25.
[26] As recommended in *Directoire*, 28.
[27] *Lumen Gentium*, 11. See also *Presbyterorum ordinis*, 5.

tions of the Word in the absence of a priest must not constitute a pillow of laziness that hinders us from being occupied with finding remedies for the lack of priests, especially in mission countries.

A community that worthily celebrates the Word must also be able to celebrate the Eucharist as worthily. "Those who preside in the Church are those who preside at Eucharist." Such was the rule of the first centuries[28] Can it again become the rule?

THE CELEBRATION OF A BIBLICAL CHURCH

With a great deal of enthusiam, Vatican II affirmed that the liturgy "shows the Church to those outside as a sign raised among the nations."[29] This affirmation fills us with joy and makes us dream of a liturgy which would be a radiant epiphany of a biblical Church. It also fills us with anguish, for we remember the insipidity of certain liturgies that are bogged down in boredom, and we ask what signs are they raising among the nations?

Joy in the Liturgy

Let us remember the homily Jesus gave on the sabbath in the synagogue of Nazareth. Luke reports that he read the prophecy of the Servant of Yahweh according to the Book of Isaiah:

The Spirit of the Lord is upon me,
for he has anointed me,
he has sent me to announce
the Good News to the poor
to proclaim deliverance to captives
and sight to the blind,
to announce to the oppressed deliverance,
to proclaim a year of grace from the Lord (Luke 4:18-19).

But Luke stops precisely before announcing vengeance: "(To proclaim) a day of vengeance for our God" (Isa 61:2b). In conformity

[28] See H.-M. Legrand, "The Presidency of the Eucharist according to the Ancient Tradition" in *Living Bread, Saving Cup*, Ed., R. Kevin Seasoltz. Collegeville, The Liturgical Press, 1982.
[29] *Sacrosanctum Concilium*, 2, citing Isa 11:12.

with his theology and his personal options,[30] Luke presents the celebration of the Good News as the feast of God's joy on the earth.

In conformity with the Jewish tradition, Luke considers the homily itself as a "word of consolation" (*logos parakleseos*). Thus when the leaders of the synagogue at Antioch of Pisidia invite Paul to give the homily after the reading of the Law and the Prophets, during the Sabbath office, the leaders tell him: "Brothers, if you have some words of consolation (*logos parakleseos*) to say, speak."[31] The word *paraklesis* or "consolation" can signify homily: thus Timothy is invited to consecrate himself "to the reading (the Scriptures), to the consolation (the homily) and to teaching."[32]

All liturgy is a meeting place with the joy of God. "Come with songs of joy,"[33] says the psalmist. The liturgy of the Word, especially, creates a community of joy. It is good that Jesus affirms: "I said this to you that your joy may be complete."[34] In the midst of the deepest distress, the faithful can experience what Paul calls magnificently "the consolation of the Scriptures."[35]

The kingship psalms (Pss 96–98) affirm that at the coming of the Lord the trees of the forest will dance for joy, the rivers will clap their hands, the mountains will skip with joy, the sea and all it contains will exult before the face of the Lord. Each liturgical celebration is like a descent of the Eternal into our time, like an appeal of the Word in our silence, like an erruption of God's infinite joy into our sadness. Each celebration of the Word must be in harmony with the cries of joy of the mountains, the dances of the trees of the forest, the trickling of the rivers as they clap their hands.

It is not a question of giving oneself trouble to find this joy, by saying over and over again: "Let us rejoice sisters and brothers!" For joy will spring up from every liturgy in the measure that it is celebrated in truth. Where God reigns, joy triumphs. Where God is celebrated, happiness blossoms. And if we do not perceive the dance of the trees of the forest, nor the cries of joy of the hills, it is simply the sign of our deafness and of our hardness, for near to

---

[30] See L. Deiss, *Synopse*, Desclée de Brouwer, 1975, 268.
[31] Acts 13:15.
[32] 1 Tim 4:13.
[33] Ps 100:2.
[34] John 16:14.
[35] Rom 15:4 (referring to 1 Macc 12:9 and 2 Macc 15:9).

God all is joy. Joy is one of the most manifest signs of the authenticity of our liturgical celebrations.

The beauty of the liturgy

Another sign that the biblical Church can raise up among the nations is the beauty of its liturgy. The rubrics wish to surround the celebration of the Word, especially that of the Gospel, with an environment of beauty. They call for a Book of the Gospels worthy of the Word of God, an ambo, the table of the Word, that responds by its beauty to the altar, the table of the Eucharist. They call for a procession "like the power of Christ triumphant over death," as the first *Ordo* said, which goes from the altar to the ambo, accompanied by candles, incense, and the singing of the Alleluia. The flowers that accompany the Word must not be unworthy.

It is necessary to know what the Missal directs. It is normal to try to carry this out obediently. It is wise to invent new forms to embellish the liturgy. Certainly the demons of aestheticism seek unceasingly, under the pretext of embellishment, to chain us to the admiration of vain beauty, to align our liberty in the shackles of ritualism. There is danger that the choir may make us drunk with its chords and rhythms (whether they are classical polyphony, modern chant, or Gregorian chant) instead of singing an Alleluia in unison with the assembly. There is the danger of architecture which makes a grandiose display instead of indicating a fully functional ambo and altar. There is the danger of a priest disguised as a prince of an operetta and of choir children dressed as dolls, instead of displaying the primal beauty of being dressed in prayer robes. The Missal speaks with reason of this "noble simplicity that is the perfect companion of genuine art.[36] Beauty is the sister of simplicity.

Beauty is also the path to God. It is not God's house where we should live forever. It is a sign of tenderness to draw us toward God, the source of all marvels. The perfume of the rose is lent to us, as is the smile of the child. The song of the nightingale is lent to us, as is the grace of a young girl. We are not owners of these beauties. We cannot keep them for ourselves, no more than we can catch a ray of the moon in the palm of our hand, or hook ourselves up to the neck of the wind. The bread of the earth is also lent to

[36] *GIRM*, 287. Cf. also 312.

us in order that we should consecrate it into the bread of heaven, into the Eucharist, into praise of God on the earth. Such is the vocation of all created beauty at the heart of our liturgical celebrations.

Certain celebrations after Vatican II have lacked beauty. There is an urgent need to fill this deficit. N. Berdiaev (†1948) affirmed that "beauty will save the world."[37] It will also save our liturgies. It is an urgent necessity.

The prayer of the body and of the soul

No religion venerates the body as much as the Christian religion: it celebrates it as the temple of the Holy Spirit, it promises it resurrection in the glory of heaven. No tradition associates it more with the liturgical celebration than the Judeo-Christian tradition. Nowhere are we invited with so much insistence:

> Lift up hands towards the sanctuary,
> bless the Lord! (Ps 134:2)

Nowhere are we pushed with so much urgency to applaud the wholly spiritual God:

> All peoples clap your hands
> cry to God with shouts of joy (Ps 47:2).

Nowhere are we asked so sustainedly to go before him with cries of joy, to prostrate ourselves in his presence, to kneel before him:

> Come, cry out with joy to the Lord,
> Come before him giving thanks,
> acclaim him to the sound of music.
> Enter, bow and bend low,
> Let us kneel before the God who made us (Ps 95:1-2, 6).

Nowhere are we invited to dance so much around his altar:

> I dance around your altar
> singing a song of thanksgiving,
> proclaiming all your wonders (Ps 26:6-7).

---

[37] N. Berdiaev, *Destin de l'homme dans le monde actuel* (Paris, 1936) 318. Cited by M.-M. Davy, "La Mystique du monde nouveau," in *Encyclopédie des Mystiques*, Éd. Laffont, 1972, 426.

Nowhere are so many musical instruments—trumpet, harp, zither, tamborine, strings, pipes, cymbals—brought together to orchestrate the dance in his honor:

> Praise him with the sound of the trumpet,
> Praise him with the zither and harp,
> Praise him with the dance and the tamborine
> Praise him with strings and pipes,
> Praise him with resounding cymbals
> Praise him with triumphant cymbals (Ps 150:3-5).

We may recognize that these calls of the Word of God have not always been fully heard. According to biblical revelation, human beings—body and soul—are the masterwork of creation, and it is in the unity of body and soul that they must adore their Creator. Yet our celebrations have sometimes been so intellectualized, so disincarnate, that they have practically banished the body from sharing in this adoration. Hellenism (Stoicism, Pythagorianism, Platonism) has invaded the human conscience and has thrown suspicion on the human body, sometimes banishing it from Christian worship. According to Plato, the body is the prison that holds the soul captive, which soils it, which stops it from being concerned with divine realities, except as through the grille of a prison.[38] It is explained—but without justifying it—that Christians, seduced by the splendor of certain Platonist themes and influenced by its dualism, have shown little eagerness to invite "the prison of the soul" to sing to their Creator. We have sometimes preferred the philosophy of Plato to the message of the Word of God.

Our industrialized societies are also marked by utilitarianism. A person is worth what he or she produces. *Homo festivus* (the festive human being), the one who sings "for nothing," simply because his or her heart marvels at the love of God, is easily suspected of fantasizing, if not of psychic unbalance. We say that the saints worked a lot. We do not say that they laughed a lot, still less that they danced a lot for God. We tend rather to affirm that they were so devout that they renounced dancing for ever.

The waves of this utilitarianism have invaded the liturgy, even that renewed by Vatican II. Laughter is excluded, joy is rather rare.

---

[38] Platon, *Phédon*, 82–83. See the good introductions to these problems in "Hellénisme et Spiritualité patristiques" of P.-T. Camelot, in *Dict. de Spiritualité*, vol. 7, col. 145–164, and "Platonisme" of A. Solignac, *op. cit.*, vol. 12, col. 1803–1811.

Our Sunday Masses, instead of expressing the joy of encountering the risen Christ, often show forth Christians who are accomplishing a useful task, a Sunday duty, which will help them get to heaven. On the level of rubrics, everything is executed according to the ritual directions. Only one thing is lacking: the joy of faith, wonder in the presence of God's beauty. They do not succeed in throwing off the yoke of sadness. It is not for nothing that young people avoid or ignore the liturgy: the *re-form* of the liturgy does not interest them (they did not know the liturgy before the Council), it is the present *form* that they judge. The level of practice among Christians has dropped by 50 percent in the last twenty years. When dioceses notice that the number of Christians is increasing while the number of people who "practice" is diminishing, we are obliged to admit that there is a problem.

What to do today?

The Catholic community represents 17.64 percent of the world's population.[39] Billions of people surround us, sometimes spying on us. What to do?

Certain communities continue tranquilly along their path of biblical and liturgical torpor, as if there were no urgency to confront. We must let them die in peace.

Certain communities radiate hope. They say: "We do not wish to die!" and they make admirable efforts to truly become the Church according to the Word of God. They know well that no song and no dance will suffice to realize this ideal, but they try to live fully according to the Word of God in order to harvest joy and beauty, with canticles and songs as a bonus.

We have the most marvellous God to manifest to the world, the most sublime revelation to proclaim, the most spiritual liturgy, but also the most incarnate, to celebrate.

We must become the Church of which the prophet says:

> I am going to create Jerusalem joy
> and her people, gladness (Isa 65:18).

We must become the new Jerusalem, clothed with God's own beauty:

---

[39] According to the agency FIDES, in *Doc. Cath.*, 1989, 29.

Yahweh will be your eternal light
and your God will be your beauty (Isa 60:20).

As for the dance, it must never cease in the Church, since God himself leads it:

He will renew you in his love,
He will dance for you with cries of joy
as on days of festival (Soph 3:17).

Billions of sisters and brothers ask us: "Where is joy?" "Where is the beauty of God on the earth?" "Where are the dances and the tamborines?" May we be able to reply to them: "Come with us and see!"